CLICK))))
your way
to **RALLY**
Obedience

Pamela S. Dennison

Alpine
PUBLICATIONS

P.O. Box 7027, Loveland, CO • www.alpinepub.com

Click Your Way to Rally Obedience

ISBN 13: 978-1-57779-108-9
ISBN 10: 1-57779-108-8

The use of APDT and AKC rally signs in this book does not constitute endorsement of the text or any of the methods herein by either APDT or AKC. All information contained in this book is complete and accurate to the best of our knowledge. Recommendations are made without guarantee on the part of the author or Alpine Publications, Inc. The author and publisher disclaim any liability with the use of this information.

This book is available at special quantity discounts for breeders and for club promotions, premiums, or educational use. Write for details.

For the sake of simplicity, the terms "he" or "she" are sometimes used to identify an animal or person. These are used in the generic sense only. No discrimination of any kind is intended toward either sex.

Many manufacturers secure trademark rights for their products. When Alpine Publications is aware of a trademark claim, we identify the product name by using initial capital letters.

Cover Design: Kelly Hines Keller, GrafikNature Design
Cover Photo: Judith Strom
Editing: Deborah Helmers
Layout: GrafikNature Design
Photographs by the author unless otherwise indicated

1 2 3 4 5 6 7 8 9 0

Printed in the United States of America

DEDICATED TO SOME OF THE BEST:

U-CD Commander Cody's Great Escape (Cody),
CGC, A-CD, CDX, NJC, R1MCL
October 18, 1992–June 6, 2005

A/C CH Bastion's Ruff Rider O'Waters (Ted),
CGC, TDI, OA, CD, RS-1, NJC, S-NAC, JS-1, HIC, ROM, R1MCL
June 6, 1995–July 19, 2005

Stonehill's Temptress (Gretchen),
NJC, NJC-V, NAC-V, TDIAOV, HIC, HT, A-CD, R1CL, R2MCL
July 22, 1995–February 1, 2005

TABLE OF CONTENTS

ACKNOWLEDGMENTS

Many thanks go to Charles "Bud" Kramer for coming up with the idea for Rally obedience in the first place and to Y2K9's in Pennsylvania for offering the Rally seminar that hooked me in. My everlasting gratitude goes to Patty Ruzzo and Leslie Nelson, who both taught me so much about positive training for competition. A big thank-you also goes to Judges Ali Brown, Linda Sperco, Sue Oakes and Betsy Baird for making sure my facts on rules were correct. And much appreciation for the dogs (and people) that posed for this book:

Stacey Herman Modica, Greater Swiss Mountain Dog (Codi)
Drumhill-Mt Airy Third X Charm, CGC, RL1

Andrea Kelly, Bull Mastiff (Quigley)
CH Banshee's Bastion Fitzwaters

Andrea Kelly, Bull Mastiff (Darcy)
CH Bastion's Banshee Riverdance, RN

Andrea Kelly, Bull Mastiff (Flute)
CH Banshee's Watersford Crystal OAP, NJP, CD, RE, WDV-2, WDO-1, HIC, RL2, RLV, AOE
8/22/01 - 5/30/10

Jane Killion, Bull Terrier (Ruby)
CH Corsaire Carpe Diem of Madcap, VA, NAP, NJP, NAC, CGC, TT

Anna Burbank, Papillon (Belle)
Jaymar Fancy Tinkerbelle

Anna Burbank, Italian Greyhound/
American Staffordshire Mix (Po Anne)

Briget Burbank, Papillon (Tuffy)
Sherjak's Ruff 'n Tuff, OA, OAJ, EAC, EJC, TN-O, TG-N

Molly Burbank, Papillon (Sempkin)
Sherjak's Semper Fidelis, NA, OAJ, EAC, EJC, NGC, TN-O, TG-N

Pamela Dennison, Border Collie (Beau) ARCHEX Surely Ewe Beau
Jest, CGC, TDI, CD, A-UD, NAP, NAJP, TSW

Pamela Dennison, Border Collie (Shadow) ARCHEX Ewe Are Beyond
a Shadow of a Doubt, CGC, A-CD, NA, NAJ, TSW

Thanks to Judith Crow, Virginia Wind and Andrea Kelly for taking
some of the photos.

Special thanks to my friend and agent Jacky Sach, to Deborah Helmers,
editor extraordinaire, and to Meg Irizarry, assistant extraordinare.

INTRODUCTION

Rally Obedience has been a titling event through the Association of Pet Dog Trainers (APDT) since September 2001. The American Kennel Club (AKC) added Rally to its roster of dog sports on January 1, 2005. Here's an amazing statistic: In the AKC alone, in the first eight months of Rally being a titling event, 8,912 dogs were entered in 658 Rally trials! Compare that to the first year agility was accepted by the AKC: only 23 trials and 2,000 entries. Pretty remarkable!

I *love* Rally. I utilize many of the Rally moves in my pet classes as well as in my aggressive dog classes. The behaviors learned are wonderful for living in the real world, with real dogs and real life scenarios, and can be instrumental in getting you and your dog out of real danger. The come front, about turn, about U turn, moving side step right, moving down, fast forward from a sit and attention heeling can become part of your regular training, whether you are an instructor or a dog owner.

Competing in Rally is fun and enhances the human/dog bond like no other sport. You are encouraged to talk to your dog throughout the course. In agility you are running so fast to keep up with your dog (at least I am) that you haven't much breath left for interacting with him, while in competition obedience, you are only allowed to talk between exercises.

Learning often is more fun with a specific purpose in mind, and Rally is a worthwhile goal. Aim for that goal, but plan on a pleasant surprise. These exercises will not simply be valuable to you in the show ring, they will greatly enhance your day-to-day routine with your dog.

chapter

1

INTRODUCTION TO RALLY

The handler moves quickly, stepping to the right, to the left, circling, halting, and then taking off again. Her dog, his eyes glued to her face, almost magically stays by her side, shadowing her every move. She is smiling widely; his tail wags constantly as his body quivers with excitement—clearly they are both having the time of their lives. Where are they? *At a Rally trial.*

Rally Obedience was initially developed in 2000 by Charles "Bud" Kramer, who was also the innovator of the first American agility program back in 1984. Over the years, Kramer had watched interest in competition obedience decline. To attract new people to the sport of dogs, he came up with the idea for a sport with a "softer" climate than traditional competition obedience, one that more enhanced the human/dog bond. And so Rally was born. The sport has often been described as a mixture of agility and competition obedience. This is because some of the behaviors in Rally are similar to behaviors used in competition obedience, but as in agility, participants in Rally follow a numbered course—the judge doesn't call a pattern.

When competing in Rally, you essentially follow a course of signs and perform the behavior(s) listed on each card. The judge does not follow you too closely, just near enough to score you. You are on your own once you say "Ready!" You complete the course at your own speed and you can talk to your dog the entire time if you wish.

Being originally a "snob" competition person, when Rally first came out I thought it was stupid. That lasted right up until I actually went to a Rally seminar. Within ten minutes, I was completely and utterly hooked. Rally Obedience (whether the AKC (American Kennel Club) or APDT (Association of Pet Dog

Trainers) venue) is a wonderful sport that utilizes many different behaviors. Some of these behaviors are used in competition obedience, and some are wonderful for just plain, day-to-day living with your dog. Passing other dogs or people on the road or trail, getting around a show site, even taking your dog to a flea market will all be easier, more enjoyable and safer if your dog knows the Rally moves outlined in this book.

REASONS TO COMPETE IN RALLY

Rally is all about having fun and interacting with your dog while competing for titles. If you enjoy training your dog and want to take that training past the basics or if you are wondering what a good next step would be after the Canine Good Citizen (CGC) certificate, Rally is a wonderful sport to train for. Although you don't have to have your CGC to compete, it is important that your dog knows and is proficient at loose leash walking and ignoring other dogs and also that he is responsive to some basic cues such as come, sit, down and stay. Even if your dog is just beginning to learn these things, you can start Rally training—this book is laid out in easy-to-follow, step-by-step exercises for the beginner on up.

Trialing can be scary for the new (and not-so-new) competitor. Rally is a fantastic way for both you and your dog to get used to the show scene and to take your training to new heights of proficiency. Once you have completed your Rally title(s), it is quite easy to segue into any other dog sport you may be interested in pursuing—be it competition obedience, agility, carting, or tracking, to name just a few.

The AKC and other venues are cracking down on unruly dogs that compete in agility and have been issuing non-qualifying scores to those dogs that are not under their handler's control. So while you don't need agility training to do Rally, you do need some of the basic training used in Rally to do agility.

HOW RALLY DIFFERS FROM COMPETITION OBEDIENCE

In competition obedience you are allowed to talk to your dog only between exercises. The patterns followed are very similar, if not identical, no matter which judge you show under. The judge follows at a very close distance and calls out instructions such as "right turn," "left turn," "about turn" and "halt." In AKC, ASCA (Australian Shepherd Club of America) and UKC (United Kennel Club) competition obedience (Novice), the heeling pattern is done on leash, then again off leash with a stand for exam in between (with direct contact between the judge and your dog). Once this is completed, there is an off leash recall. At the end are group stays with a one-minute sit stay in a group of approximately eleven other dogs and a three-minute down stay in that same group of dogs. Take a look at the chart below to see how competition obedience behaviors relate to Rally.

	AKC Obedience (Novice)	AKC Rally (Novice)	APDT Rally (level 1)
Heel on leash	yes	yes	yes
Heel off leash	yes	no	no
Figure 8	yes	no	no
Stand for exam	yes	no	no
Recall	yes	no	no
Group stays	yes	no	no

Of course, Rally requires many behaviors that competition obedience does not.

TRAINING WITH POSITIVE METHODS

One of the major objectives of the sport of Rally is that the dog and handler team be just that, a *team* working together in a happy and joyful manner, showing off the bond and training between them. That lighthearted relationship can only be present in the ring when it exists at home. I firmly believe in using only positive methods when working with a dog. Training Rally behaviors to precision using positive reinforce-

One of my students, Stacy, has a Greater Swiss Mountain Dog—not one of the "typical" obedience breeds you'll see competing. At his first-ever trials, Codi earned his Rally level 1 title with scores of 193, 196 and 201, and an Award of Excellence for having his first three qualifying scores 190 or higher! (I could mention that my own dogs consistently get scores of 200 or above, but then you'd think, "Yes, but those are Border Collies!")

ment will not only result in a better relationship with your dog and a dog that loves to compete, but also will yield you the same high scores as traditional training methods.

It is very important to train your dog so that he can *experience success without the fear of making a mistake*. This is achieved by breaking down each behavior into tiny pieces (approximations). The smaller the approximation, the easier it becomes to teach the "big" behavior. It is crucial to know how to break each behavior down into steps that your dog finds manageable and understandable so he can figure out just what he is being taught. I have reduced the exercises in this book in this way. Every time your dog is successful at learning one of these small steps, you keep his interest and, more importantly, build his confidence.

You want your dog to be as successful as he can be, and your training should be geared to that end goal. However, although you will always try to set the dog up to be right, there are times when he will give you a "wrong" response. In these cases, you should not be in a hurry to "fix" him, but instead should give him some time to think. Only by sampling other behaviors can your dog find out exactly what gets him reinforcement. In positive training, failure is not necessarily bad; rather, it teaches the dog what works and what doesn't.

For instance, when I watch someone training the left finish (see Chapter 3), I often see what I call a "two-part" finish. Here's what happens: The handler signals the dog to do the left finish and the dog does it crooked. The handler then signals again, the dog straightens himself and the handler rewards the dog. If repeated often enough, the dog will think this is what he is supposed to do—be crooked on the first attempt and then fix it.

The correct way to handle this is for the handler to simply stand still and wait. And wait. If the dog starts to fix himself, even if it isn't perfect, then the handler should click and treat for the attempt.

My dog Beau was nearly at the point of learning that erroneous two-part finish. I decided to see what would happen if I just stood still and did nothing after his first try. I signaled Beau to finish and he was indeed crooked. He was very attentive and I could see the wheels turning, so I grit my teeth and didn't re-signal him or help him in any way. After two minutes (yes, two minutes!), he fixed himself. I gave him a huge jackpot of treats and play.

On the other hand, you want your dog to experience as much success as possible—too much failure can create an aggressive, frustrated or quitter dog. If your dog is regularly failing, then training has probably been pushed too far, too fast.

He may be tired or not in the mood that day or you may be drilling him too much or not making the steps small enough. You also may have changed your signals without meaning to, thus causing some confusion. Training is an art, and you will need to develop a feel for when you need to make a step easier for your dog to understand and when you should allow him to "fail," thereby giving him the chance to think the problem through.

Training for any sport should be teamwork and fun for *both* of you. The joy you bring to training will shine through in the ring. For those of you who would like to read further on positive training, see Appendix 3.

BASIC DIFFERENCES BETWEEN AKC AND APDT RALLY

AKC and APDT use slightly different signs and behaviors for the various Rally levels in their venues. These differences are discussed in later chapters. For ease in training, this book is laid out so that similar exercises—regardless of venue or level—are grouped together. Each exercise is numbered in accordance with APDT and AKC Rally specifications; these numbers correspond to the numbers on each individual sign.

The basic scoring is also slightly different in the two venues. The actual judging of each exercise is not much discussed in these pages unless it has a distinct bearing on teaching the particular behavior or unless it is necessary to describe some fundamental difference between the two venues. You can go to each venue's website to see exact scoring guidelines. (Website resources for further information on each particular venue are listed in Appendix 3.)

APDT RALLY

In APDT Rally, food may be used as a reward, however you may use food only at specific signs. Watch for the words "food allowed" in the discussion in these pages. The exact timing of delivering the treats is also covered. Chapter 9 gives you more information about how to properly use food, if you so choose.

APDT Rally requires that dogs be handled by their owners or members of the owner's immediate family. There are two types of classes, A and B. A is for the *dog* that has not completed a level 1, 2 or 3 title. For instance, if you have three dogs and want to get Rally level 1, 2 or 3 titles on all of them, you would continue to show in the A classes for all of your dogs. If you want to start going for your ARCH (APDT Rally Championship) or each level's Excellent title for a particular dog, you would enter into the B class as soon as that dog earned his title in the A class. In the A classes, in case of a tie for a placement (first through fifth), there will be an actual course runoff to determine the winner—usually consisting of the first six signs of the course you just ran. In the B classes, a tying score will be resolved by the fastest time. All runs in both the A and B classes are timed. You are allowed four minutes to complete a course.

AKC RALLY

AKC Rally does not allow food in the ring. All runs are timed, although at the time of the printing of this book, there is no time limit for completing your run. Ties for placement ribbons (first through fourth) are broken by time only. There are no runoffs unless there is a tie for time as well as score. A runoff in this case consists of rerunning a full course.

AKC also has A and B classes; however, the distinctions are made along different lines than in APDT. For AKC Novice level, if you as a *handler* have achieved any other AKC Rally title with another dog or any AKC competition obedience title with any dog, you must enter into the B classes. The A classes are for handlers and dogs that have never earned an AKC Rally title (RN) or any AKC Novice, Open or Utility title. Handlers must own the dog entered or be a member of the owner's household or immediate family.

In the Advanced and Excellent levels, the distinction is slightly different. If the *dog* you are showing presently in Rally has an AKC Novice, Open or Utility title, you must show in the B classes. If you have titled a previous dog in AKC Novice, Open or Utility, but are now showing in AKC Rally a dog that doesn't have those titles, you may enter into the A classes. The owner or any other person may handle dogs in the B classes in these two levels.

RALLY LEVELS

APDT Rally has three levels:

- Rally level 1 (title designation RL1), performed on leash
- Rally level 2 (title designation RL2), performed off leash
- Rally level 3 (title designation RL3), performed off leash

APDT also offers Individual Level Championship titles (adding an "X" after the titles shown above), Rally Champion (ARCH), Rally Champion Excellent (ARCHX), Rally Champion Extraordinaire (ARCHEX), Rally Master Champion (ARCHMX) titles. More information about the specific requirements for each title is listed in Appendix 1.

AKC Rally also has three levels:

- Rally Novice (title designation RN), performed on leash
- Rally Advanced (title designation RA), performed off leash
- Rally Excellent (title designation RE), performed off leash

AKC also offers a Rally Advanced Excellent title (RAE). More information about the specific requirements for each title is listed in Appendix 1.

Try not to let yourself get too bogged down with the distinctions listed here—this will only put your mind into information overload, and you may want to quit before even starting. Relax, train the behaviors needed, learn what the signs mean and the rest will fall into place. **Above all, have fun.**

RALLY AROUND

- You don't need a CGC in order to compete in Rally, but knowing some simple behaviors beforehand will be very helpful for you and will make the training go faster.
- In both AKC and APDT Rally, verbal praise from the handler is encouraged throughout the course.
- Of the two venues, APDT is the one that allows you to use food in the ring as a reward.

chapter

2

RALLY RUDIMENTS

Before you can start training for Rally, you will need to train a few base behaviors, including, in particular, rapt attention from your dog. Attention is the cornerstone of Rally. I am not talking about forced attention from your dog, but a willing focus amidst a myriad of distractions. Skip the basics and you will not be successful in the exercises outlined in this book. Take the time now, and the benefits will be enormous in both Rally and real life.

CLICKER TRAINING IN A NUTSHELL

The clicker is an extremely powerful tool. You might wonder how this little plastic noisemaker can have such a profound effect on your dog's behavior. How is it that the once impenetrable communication barrier between human and canine can be overcome with such a seemingly simplistic method?

Assuming that your dog has never heard its sound before, the clicker can be considered a neutral stimulus; that is, in the beginning, the noise itself has no meaning, conveys no message and conjures no emotions or feelings. It means absolutely nothing. Your dog is then conditioned (taught) that something wonderful (to him) will always follow the sound of the click. The clicker also communicates to your dog exactly which specific behavior is "right"—it is very clear to your dog what behavior you are marking. Another important point is that the clicker sounds the same each and every time you use it.

You may certainly use a verbal marker such as "good" or "yes"; however, because your dog is exposed to the sound of "humanspeak" throughout his day-to-day life with you, your language becomes, to a certain degree, white noise. If you are like many dog owners, you talk to your spouse and children, conduct marathon phone conversations, sing in the shower and perhaps talk to yourself. Maybe you even talk in your sleep! Add into the mix the TV and radio you leave on to soothe your companion when you are gone. Additionally, none of this banter is executed in monotones. Your language likely is peppered with inflections, emotions, modulating tones and volume changes.

Remember that your dog does not speak English, so it will be harder for him to discriminate between your talking to and around him all day long and your verbal marker. Think of how many variations of "good" or "yes" you can come up with—soft, loud, happy, angry—the possibilities are endless. Conversely, that little clicker always remains exactly the same. If utilized properly, once your dog knows what the sound means, there will be no doubt in his mind what you are telling him.

Now, before you panic and think that once you start using the clicker, you will be forever conjoined with that piece of plastic or that you won't be able to compete (since clickers are not allowed in Rally) because your dog can't perform without it—it absolutely isn't true. The clicker is used only in the beginning stages of training each exercise to impart valuable information from you to your dog.

For instance, sit is a very easy behavior for most dogs. Usually within two to three days, you will be able to say "sit" and your dog will sit. You can then wean your dog off the clicker as a marker for that behavior; he will still sit when you ask him to and won't expect a treat for each and every sit.

If you click, you must reinforce in some way—be it with food, toys, petting, praise or play. If a reward does not follow, the click loses meaning for your dog. To wean a dog off the clicker once a behavior is learned, you simply ask for the behavior and not click when you get it—perhaps as a transition you praise him instead, or maybe you simply go on to the next behavior. Alternatively, when you are training heel, for example, you can click and treat every step to start, then every second step, every third, fifth, eighth, etc., until you are doing an entire course without using a clicker. For more information on positive and clicker training, see Appendix 3.

HOW TO BEGIN

To start, you will need to make the clicker valuable and meaningful to your dog. To do this, have your dog in front of you, and armed with a handful of food, you click and treat, click and treat, click and treat. Keep up a nice steady pace, and continue for as many times as you can in three minutes. It doesn't matter what your dog is doing (as long as he isn't jumping or barking); just click and treat. Be sure that the food follows within one-half second after the click. That is the optimum time for your dog to make the association that the click sound is valuable. Any longer time span between the click noise and the treat will result in your dog not making the correct association.

You may have noticed that I am not asking you to use a "watch me" cue for eye contact. If you teach this behavior correctly, you won't need the cue at all. I don't teach my own dogs that cue because they automatically watch me. I use eye contact as the requirement for almost everything: If they want the ball, they have to look at me before I'll throw it. If they want to go swimming, they have to look at me before I'll release them. If you use a "watch me" cue, your dog will only look at you because you are asking him to. Train it the way outlined here and your dog will look at you all of the time.

Most of the time, you will only have to do this step once and your dog will make the connection. If for some reason your dog doesn't understand that when he hears the click he gets a treat, simply repeat the exercise for a few more sessions of a few minutes each.

ATTENTION: PART ONE

Once your three minutes (or so) of the previous exercise are up, you will click for attentive behavior. Have your clicker in one hand and food in the other. Put your arms down by your side. (Do not have them at your waist—this will be important later on.) Wait. Don't say anything. Once the dog looks at your face (the behavior you want), click and treat. Put your arms down by your side again. Wait for eye contact and then click and treat. Repeat this for about five minutes. At this beginning stage, it doesn't matter exactly where your dog is—he can be sitting, lying down or standing. Repeat this a few times per day, a few minutes at a time. You will soon see your dog staring at you incessantly throughout the day. This is a good thing! We want him to be drilling holes in your head with his eyes.

ATTENTION: PART TWO

The second step is to make sure that your dog knows his name and will respond instantly when he hears it. *When* he looks at you (not *before* he looks at you), you say his name and then click and treat. If you say his name before he is looking at you, you are nagging (and we all know how much we like people who nag us!). If you wait until he looks at you, you are teaching. Repeat this a few minutes per session, a few short sessions per day. At this stage of the game, it doesn't matter where he is, as long as he is close to you.

ATTENTION: PART THREE

The next step is the starting point for teaching your dog what "come" means. *When* he looks at you (just as in the previous exercise), say his name, say your "come" word, and then click and treat. You are not asking him to move at this point. You just want him to listen to the words. Repeat this for a few minutes per session, a few short sessions per day.

ON THE ROAD

Now take what you have learned so far—eye contact, eye contact/name, eye contact/name/come—and go on the road. Get out of the living room and your front yard (because there will be no Rally trials held there) and practice these simple behaviors in every location you can think of: parking lots, fields, schoolyards, parks, pet stores, downtown. Be creative. If your dog is too distracted at first, go to less busy places to start, gradually adding in more and more distracting places.

Teaching the recall this way is actually called *back chaining*. **Question:** What is the last piece of a recall? **Answer:** The dog right in front of you. If you train this part first you are making the entire behavior stronger and more reliable.

After about two weeks of steady training (five minutes per session, three times per day), you should have incredible focus from your dog. You will then be able to start teaching him other behaviors.

GET THE BEHAVIOR, THEN NAME IT

When training all of the new behaviors listed in this book, be sure to pair the word with the behavior for fastest learning. This principle will apply for every behavior you will teach your dog, even if it isn't for competing. There is a real reason for the sequence of "get the behavior, *then* name it." While a dog can learn some verbal cues, spoken language is not his forte. He is more cognizant of body postures than verbal language. The dog will learn a new behavior more easily if he doesn't have to filter through extra verbiage.

To make these new behaviors easier for your dog to understand, you will split them into tiny pieces (approximations). Teaching the behavior first and only then naming it enhances learning and recognition of the word and its corresponding behavior. In the beginning of each new step, you must avoid naming a less than perfect response; otherwise, that is what you will get—a less than perfect response whenever you say that word! You want your dog to learn that the verbal cue means the finished product, not a small portion of it.

A classic example of pairing a word with the wrong behavior is this: Your dog is jumping on you as you say "off!" Do this enough, and every time you say "off" he will jump. Why? Because that is the word you have paired with jumping! If you say "off" *as* he is getting off, you are doing it correctly.

THE SIT

In Rally you need the dog to sit directly in front of you as well as on your left side in heel position. Let's start with the front sit. There is no need to yank up on the dog's neck while you push down on the hind end. Instead, have a treat in your right or left hand and, palm up, hold the treat over the dog's head, luring him so his head is up. Using canine physics (head goes up, hind end goes down), your dog will sit. Say "sit" when his

Hand signal for the sit.

Proper front position.

Proper heel position—
note the position of Quigley and
the correct body posture of Andrea.

hind end hits the ground, and then click and treat. Be sure not to say "sit" until he sits—otherwise you are giving the word "sit" to the behavior of standing.

After about three to four days, you should be able to say your cue word "sit" before the behavior and your dog should sit. If he looks at you blankly, give him a helper hand signal. Know that your dog isn't stupid. Just remember that he is more focused on your body than your words.

Practice this with the dog in front of you in proper front position. Do not lure him with your hands into position—for now, *you* go to proper front position. Let's teach him what the "right" picture looks like for now—you standing straight, the dog directly in front of you, looking adoringly into each other's eyes, with your hands down at your sides. Practice "front" for a few minutes per day during your training.

Your dog will now need to learn that the heel position is as valuable as the front position. Start with your dog in front of you. You go to heel position. Stand up straight, head pointed forward, chin slightly down (so you can look at your dog), left arm at your waist.

Click and treat him just for looking at the "right" picture. Repeat this again and again, one right after the other. Your dog may try to get into front position

A side note about **luring** and **props**: Luring is okay —to a point. I use luring in this book only when the lure becomes the actual hand signal. If you use luring or props too long and don't fade them as soon as you start to use them, you are doomed. I once saw a woman at a competition obedience trial practicing outside the ring. She was using lures to get her dog to come and sit front. Once in the ring, she was not allowed to use those lures and the dog had no clue what she wanted him to do. She then became very frustrated and angry at her dog. *Silly!*

(because he has been so heavily reinforced for this in the past). Don't get angry with him—just have him sit, you move back to heel position and try again. I like to start this training off with rapid clicks and treats because of this potential problem. Usually after a few minutes the dog will stop moving to the front as he starts learning that heel position also pays off. Make sure you are clicking and treating him for looking up at your face. For a few minutes per day, rotate practicing heel position with front position. Be sure that your posture is correct.

Practice in front of a mirror if you need to. It is important that your position be accurate because we are trying to teach the dog what the perfect picture looks like. It is harder to fix this later on than to get it correct from the beginning.

THE DOWN

Have the dog in a sit and bring your hand (slowly) straight down to the ground. *When* the dog lies down (not before), say "down" and then click and treat. Put the treat on the ground so you can then stand up straight without the dog popping up again. This may happen anyway—not to worry—just give the dog a few treats to keep him busy while you stand up. Once he is done eating the treats, release him with a verbal

Some people may think that this posture looks too militaristic—it may indeed. However, if you have a tallish dog and you heel with your arms down, you are going to whack him in the face, and I don't think he will appreciate it. If you have a short dog, your swinging arm may block his view of your face and he may go wide or forge in an attempt to see your face.

"okay" or "free." We want him to get up on *your* cue, so be sure to release him before he thinks of it himself. Repeat this bunches of times.

Luring into the down.

You will also need to fade your hand signal, which sometimes takes longer than fading the hand signal for the sit. Most of us start out luring the down by bending all the way down to the ground. Once the dog is going down quickly, you will gradually bend over less and less, still not saying "down" until your dog lies down.

Once you can stand up straight and give a small hand signal, you should be able to start saying the word "down" before the behavior. If your dog doesn't respond, use a helper hand signal cue and just try again. Be sure to practice this with your dog in front of you and also at your side in heel position.

COME

You have already started to teach your dog (by pairing the word with the click and treat) that the word "come" is valuable. Now we need to get him moving. Not only is "come" important for Rally, but it is imperative in real life as well. Pick a come word that you will remember and use consistently. Stay away from changing your come word repeatedly—it will only confuse your dog.

Be careful that you don't dilute your come word by using it for anything other than a recall. "Come" should not be used for heeling! In the beginning stages of the recall, do not say the word unless your dog is already on his way to you. You must pair the word with the behavior for the dog to learn exactly what "come" means.

- Say "come" only when you are prepared to reinforce heavily—for at least twenty seconds! If you don't have any reinforcers on you, you can run to them, all the while keeping your dog's attention on you.
- Make sure your dog comes within a few inches—do not reach out to feed him.
- Make sure that when you say "come" you say it only once. You want your dog to come to you the first time you say it, not the twentieth time.

If you have poisoned your recall word and taught your dog to run away or ignore you completely when you say it, then by all means change to a new word. "Here" works well, and I have also heard people use the word "front." Be creative, but be sure to pick a word that you and the rest of your family will remember and be consistent about using correctly this time.

RECALL GAMES

The following games are not just for Rally—they may eventually save your dog's life one day. All of these games are also great for teaching your dog to be very focused on you and will help immensely when you start to teach the heel.

HEAT-SEEKING MISSILE

Get one of your friends to hold your dog while you run away and hide. The second you say his name ("Cody, come") your friend should drop the leash. If you are training by yourself, just run and hide while he isn't looking at you. Once you are hidden, call your dog. When he finds you, have a huge party with all sorts of reinforcers, such as food, petting and playing with toys—make it a *big* deal when he finds you.

TAG, YOU'RE IT!

Run around like a bunny, feinting right and left. Your dog will most likely chase you. Reinforce him for following you. Repeat this game often, always making sure you reward him for staying with you.

NATURE WALK

Bring some toys and treats and a long leash to a nice, wide-open area and just start walking. Most likely, your dog will go on ahead. No problem. Just say his name before he hits the end of the leash. As he is coming back to you, say your come word, click and heavily reinforce him when he responds. Be sure once in a while to play the "tag, you're it" game. If you find a tree or bush, you can also hide and play the "heat-seeking missile" game.

If your dog hits the end of the leash, just stand still and wait for him to notice that you are still there. If your dog doesn't come when you call, don't call him again. Be patient and wait. You can even sit down on the ground to entice him without actually saying anything. However long it takes, you still reinforce him for coming to you. Be careful not to talk to him when he isn't doing what you want—otherwise you are actually reinforcing him for ignoring you.

When just starting out, it is best to use a harness when playing this game. That way, you avoid the dog developing tracheal, neck or spinal damage if he hits the end of the leash at full force. My favorite harnesses are listed in Appendix 3.

THE FRONT GAME

In order to practice recalls for the real world and also a nice straight front for Rally, you must start by getting your dog to go away from you so you can call him back.

The Recall

1. Toss a cookie about two or three feet away.
2. Let your dog know he can have it by saying "get it."
3. Run away fast!
4. Your dog will chase you. As he is on his way, say "come." (Be sure not to say "come" as he is eating the cookie, at least in the beginning stages of this game.)
5. When he gets to you, click and treat with a bunch of cookies fed one at a time. Be unpredictable in the number of cookies you dole out. In addition, make sure you don't always use food as the only reinforcer. Otherwise it becomes b-o-o-o-r-r-r-ing!

Why do you drop the cookie at first? For no other reason than to get a head start—after all, your dog runs much faster than you do.

Showing your dog the right picture.

Spreading your legs and tossing the treat.

The Front

Pretty soon, your dog will get the idea and you will need to throw the treat farther away to keep your head-start advantage. When you have at least five to ten feet between the two of you, show your dog the "right" picture as he is racing toward you—standing up straight, legs together, arms down at your side. At the last minute, spread your legs and toss the treat between them so that he races through them.

If you have thrown your treat far enough between your legs, you can then just turn, face your dog again, show him the right picture and repeat the process. Once you have done this at least two dozen times, pull a switch and don't spread your legs. Your dog should screech to a halt and will most likely be straight in front of you. Click and jackpot each and every time he comes in straight. If he comes in crooked, don't click, just toss.

If your dog comes in crooked anyway, just spread your legs and toss the treat through them. If he comes in closer to your right side, then step to the left and toss him through. If he comes in closer to your left, then step to the right. (If you step in the other direction, you are adjusting yourself to the dog rather than the other way around.) Be very generous when he gets it right. You can be "cheap" when he isn't straight in the beginning. After all, he did come when you called, so you still want to reinforce that. As he progresses and gets better at it, then you can raise your criteria and only click and reinforce those straight fronts that are perfect.

As noted behaviorist Ted Turner says, "when training a behavior, if you want to see a big change, make a big difference." If you give the same amount of reinforcement for a crooked recall as you do for a straight one, your dog may have a harder time figuring out what the right thing to do is.

I am feeding with my palm facing Shadow so his head remains straight. Photo: V. Wind.

When you are feeding, make sure your hand is flat, palm facing the dog. This will help keep his body straight. If you feed with your right or left hand and his nose turns toward that hand, then his hind end will have a tendency to move out of a straight front position.

Once you have taught your dog the stay (see the honor exercise in Chapter 7), you can do the recall more formally. For instance, you can ask your dog to stay, walk out approximately six to eight feet, turn and face your dog and call him to come. If you'll notice, I am not asking you to lure the dog to front position. Fading lures is a pain; additionally, lures only teach the dog to follow your hands—I use them sparingly for that reason. Work on a great deal of eye contact in front position. Most of the time if the dog is looking up at you as he comes in, he will come in straight.

ADDING DISTRACTIONS

You are going to practice all of the behaviors listed in this and subsequent chapters in varied locations. Try to do this from the very beginning of training.

The sooner your dog is comfortable with listening to you in busy places, the better off you will be when you want to start competing.

Buy a fifty-foot long line and go out and conquer. Why a fifty-foot line? The long line becomes a portable fence. You can't exercise a dog properly on a six-foot leash, and the leash is not a tool anyway, it is a safety net. If you are in a fenced-in area, by all means feel free to train off leash to start.

Be aware that the more intense the distractions, the more exciting your reinforcers must be. Start with mild distractions that are far away and gradually build to stronger, closer ones. Always set your dog up to be successful in ignoring the distractions. Train for more distractions than you expect to encounter. That way, once you are at a trial, the actual distractions will be a piece of cake for you and your dog. More information on positive proofing (that is, using positive methods to train a dog to ignore distractions) can be found in Chapter 8.

People look at me funny when I tell them that I train my own dogs—and quite a few of my students' dogs—off leash before working on leash. Because we work so hard on building a relationship/bond with our dogs, we don't need a leash to train the behaviors listed in this book. The leash doesn't control your dog—your training controls your dog.

USING REINFORCEMENTS PROPERLY

As you begin training, it is important that you understand how to use food and other types of reinforcers properly. Yes, there is a great deal of information packed into the beginning of this book, but don't let this put you off. If you are knowledgeable about these things from the start, you won't have to go back and redo exercises later, and you will actually avoid problems. A little more time spent early on will save you a ton of time later.

If you use only food to train, then your dog will only work for food—and let me tell you that is very annoying! If you use many different types of reinforcers from the get-go, your dog will be a more enthusiastic and happy camper.

Pairing the clicker with items other than food is not only possible, it is ideal. What are the benefits of this? You decrease the possibility of your dog becoming bored and increase his drive to work with you because he will never know what's coming up next! If you have a small dog, using other types of reinforcers is a must. The average toy dog, such as a Papillon or Miniature Poodle, only eats about one-quarter of a cup per day of food. If you use only food to train, your sessions can't be much longer than a few minutes.

Another benefit is that you won't have to always carry food around with you in order to train your dog. You can also use life rewards paired with the clicker. Now, instead of constantly trying to block your dog from the environment, you can take advantage of it! If you have a real problem with your dog constantly sniffing and you can't get his attention, use sniffing to your benefit. If you utilize sniffing as an occasional reinforcer for the behavior you want, your dog won't have to "steal" opportunities to do it, and believe it or not, he will pay much more attention to you.

You can be unpredictable and exciting when doling out a reinforcer. Mix up your reinforcers and deliver them in fun and interesting ways; for instance, you can toss treats or toys up in the air rather than just handing them to your dog. You will help create a dog that is more compliant to you, happier and more fulfilled because everything becomes a reward for correct behavior.

VARIABLE SCHEDULE AND TYPE OF REINFORCEMENT

A variable *type* and variable *schedule* of reinforcement gets the bests results in dog training. "Type" refers to the reinforcer itself (food, play, sniffing, etc.). "Schedule" refers to how often you hand out the reward (every time the correct behavior is performed, every fifth time, randomly, etc.)

Because we humans are creatures of habit, we tend to get a little boring when we reinforce and start acting like vending machines ("put a dollar in, get a soda"). If you go on too long with such a consistent reward schedule (also called a 1:1 ratio), and then try to go to a random schedule of reinforcement, you can create a dog that will simply walk away when he sees you have no treats on you or in your hand. He is *not* resisting you or being stubborn or stupid—you are obviously "out of order." You wouldn't keep putting money into a broken vending machine; neither will your dog.

To become more unpredictable and fun, become a slot machine. For those of you who have ever played the slots, you know how addicting they can be. So take that lesson and utilize it so you become addicting to your dog.

Let's say you are doing an entire training session, with a come front, moving down, eye contact, heeling or any number of the behaviors listed in this book. A slot machine would reward only a few of the behaviors in each sequence. Maybe out of ten steps of heeling, you reward three times. Then out of the next ten steps of heeling, you reward two times, then four, then one, then six and so on (this is a variable schedule). You can also make the rewards more diverse. Try:

- ➡ Giving an entire handful of treats
- ➡ Clapping and cheering
- ➡ Letting your dog go sniff the ground
- ➡ Teasing him with a treat
- ➡ Letting him play with a toy
- ➡ Teasing him with the toy
- ➡ Petting softly
- ➡ Petting roughly
- ➡ Running around and letting your dog chase you
- ➡ Getting down and cuddling
- ➡ Plucking grass or snow and flinging it up in the air

Be inventive and impulsive! Your dog *will* work harder for fewer and more varied reinforcers. When he has done something amazingly well—a perfectly straight sit, super heel, phenomenal disregard of the chattering squirrel that just ran by—go wild and give him a big jackpot. If you are working on a behavior that has been hard for him and "the light comes on and someone is now home," by all means heavily reward that as well. Even the easier behaviors should once in a while reap a reinforcement bonanza. Remember, your dog is working with you, not because he *must*, but because you are making it valuable for him. He doesn't care about the ribbons or titles; he cares about having fun.

RELATING TO RALLY

Now that you have some basics under your belt and for a few weeks have been practicing all of these behaviors—eye contact, name recognition, come word recognition, sit in front position, sit in heel position, down next to you and recall games—it's time to start relating them specifically to Rally.

RALLY AROUND

- Keep your sessions short and different every time.

- Train for approximately three to four sessions per day, three to five minutes per session. End before the dog gets tired.

- Mix up the order of behaviors—don't always ask for a sit, then down, etc. Don't be predictable!

- Intersperse play into your training. Done correctly, training should be as fun as play.

- Practice in many different locations from the very beginning. You won't be sorry that you did because it will make the transition easier for you and your dog once you start competing.

- **Reinforcers** can be anything the dog wants at the time, including "life rewards" (such as eating dinner, going out for a walk, playing, getting attention, etc.). If your dog consistently tunes you out, change your reinforcer. If you like Cheerios, but love lobster, which would you work harder for? Although I do use food to train my dogs, I don't use food exclusively and am a fanatic against fat dogs. If necessary, cut down on your dog's regular food intake so he will not gain weight. When you start training, your dog may experience some diarrhea; to avoid this, gradually introduce your training treats in with his regular dinner so his system will adapt more readily to the treats.

- When used, food should be a *reward*, not a bribe or a lure.

- Your dog will perform better if he doesn't receive food for every correct behavior. Be a slot machine, not a vending machine!

- Be sure to build up the value of other types of reinforcers. You won't always have food with you.

chapter

◄ **3** ►

BASIC MANEUVERS

You will see that I am going to be very particular about your body postures and footwork in teaching Rally behaviors. Why? Because, as you will learn, certain body positions become cues to your dog to do specific things. If your body isn't placed correctly, your dog will not respond the way you want him to.

When teaching Rally, I like to teach little snippets of behaviors from different areas, rather than teaching each complete behavior as a unit. I find this to be more interesting and less like "drilling" for both the dog and handler. For instance, I start teaching with the stand, the finishes, the first few steps of heeling and the beginning steps of turns. You may feel you are not learning what you need, but have patience. The behaviors will eventually all fit together into cohesive units and suddenly you'll realize you are 90 percent there, with only a little more to train as a few finishing touches.

I also like to group similar exercises together. For example, right turns and about turns are similar and appear together. Left turns and left U turns are similar and also appear together.

NOSE TARGETING

I use nose targeting to teach finishes and the stand, and also just for fun. It is very simple to teach. Have your clicker and cookies in your right hand. Hold out your empty left hand in an inviting manner. Most dogs will sniff it out of curiosity. Click and treat with your right hand as soon as he sniffs or touches your left. Repeat a bunch of times. Then switch hands. Make it into a fun game, holding your hand low to the ground or high enough so that the dog has to jump up to nose target it. You can then start to bring your left hand back behind you in preparation for teaching the left finish or your right hand back behind you for the right finish. Common cue words for this behavior are "touch" or "target."

STAND

To teach the stand, have your dog on your left side, sitting in heel position. Reach in front of your dog with your right hand and bring your hand forward slightly and slowly. If you have done your homework on nose targeting, your dog should move forward and hence into the stand position. As soon as he stands, say "stand" and click and treat. Be sure that your hand is directly in front of your dog's nose and slightly lower— too much to the right or left will cause him to move his hind end off to the side. Too high and he won't stand. Don't forget our sit lesson—head goes up, hind end goes down. So for the stand, the head needs to come down slightly so the hind end can come up. You also want to make

The wrong way to lure into a stand —see, Darcy is still sitting.

The correct way to lure into a stand.

sure you move your hand parallel to the ground and slightly lower than his nose.

If for some reason your dog is having a hard time with this, you can place a treat between your fingers (keeping your hand flat) and lure him forward for a few repetitions. Then go back to doing the same hand signal without the food. Be sure to get that treat in at nose level to further reinforce the stand and then release him forward—otherwise your dog may have a tendency to sit again.

THE FINISHES

For both the right and left finish, it is very important that you keep your body posture (head, shoulders and waist) straight and your feet planted on the ground. If you have a toy dog, you may use a target stick in the beginning if you think you need it. Train nose targeting of the stick the same way you would have done with your hand. Present the stick and click him when he sniffs it. After teaching the finish, fade the stick by making it smaller and smaller as quickly as you can. Make sure the motion of the stick is exactly same as the motion that your empty hand will make.

Anna is using a target stick for Belle. If she had tried to use her hand to start this behavior, her body posture would have been all wrong.

LEFT FINISH

With your dog in front of you, bring your left hand (palm flat, facing your dog), straight back as far as your arm can reach (even if you have a small dog).

Once your dog is following your hand and he is all the way back, turn your hand around and lure him forward and up so he is sitting in heel position. It is important to make sure your dog goes back as far as your arm reaches because otherwise he may have a tendency to cut the corner short and be crooked on the finish. If for some reason your dog hesitates to go back all the way, you can break this down into even smaller steps. Click and treat him for going as far back as your arm can go and toss the treat behind you to further reinforce that position. You will eventually fade this huge signal to be a smaller one.

Left palm back as far as it will go. Obviously, this will be a bigger movement for a bigger dog.

And now back to heel position.

If you are having a problem with your dog following your hand, I will allow you to "cheat" for a few repetitions and have a treat in your hand. Be sure to keep your hand flat and put the treat between your fingers. That way, once you fade the food, the hand signal will remain the same.

Practice this exercise both on and off leash. In the first level in both Rally venues, you need to know how to handle the leash without dropping it or letting it get tangled.

RIGHT FINISH

Start the right finish off leash because it takes some coordination to handle the leash properly and smoothly. Once your dog is doing the finish perfectly, you can add the leash. Put a treat in each hand. With your dog in front of you and using your right hand, lure him back with your flat hand behind you and give your dog the treat (you don't click here).

Then reach around with your left hand and lure the dog forward and into heel position with your left hand. Click and treat. (No, you really don't need three hands for this.)

Right hand goes back...   ...left hand picks up the dog...

Repeat this about five to ten times and then get rid of the treat in your right hand, while continuing to give the same signal. When the dog is behind you looking for the treat, reach back with your left hand and bring him into heel position.

Repeat this about five to ten times. Then stop reaching behind you and see if, with the same right hand signal, your dog will come all the way around to heel position. You may have to lure him to help him to sit perfectly straight the first few times.

Don't name the right and left finishes until they are perfect. As I mentioned before, if you name a substandard behavior, then that is what you'll

...and lures him into heel position.

Photos: V. Wind.

Sempkin is crooked,
due to improper luring.

Jane has changed the leash from left
to right hand and is giving Ruby the
signal to go around.

Jane is picking up the leash with her
left hand once Ruby has committed
to go around.

get. The most common cue words for the left finish are "get close," "get back," and "side." The most common cue words for the right finish are "around," and "swing." You don't have to actually name these if you don't want to—you can simply use your hand signal.

You may want to practice in front of a mirror. That way you can judge accurately if your dog is straight without distorting your body and thus changing your body cues. Only click and treat the straight finishes. If you click and treat any and all attempts, your dog won't know what you really want. If your dog is coming in crooked more than two to three times in a row, then your luring needs to be adjusted. Make sure your body posture—head, neck and shoulders—is straight.

ADDING THE LEASH TO THE RIGHT FINISH

Your dog will be in front of you. Put the leash in your right hand *before* giving the right hand signal. If you switch the leash after you give the signal, your dog will get confused and not do the finish. Give your right hand signal.

Once your dog commits to going behind you, reach back with your left hand and grab the leash. You may want to practice this a few times without your dog so that it is a smooth movement.

LIFE DOESN'T ALWAYS GO IN A STRAIGHT LINE

RIGHT TURN

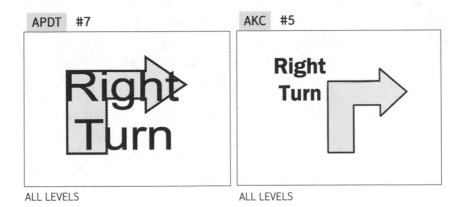

I am turning my head and shoulders to the right as Shadow follows those cues.

Right turn footwork: I am starting to look in the direction I am going.

Photos: V. Wind.

To start training the right turn, let's teach your dog that if your head and left shoulder turn away from him, that means you are going to the right.

Have your dog next to you, either sitting or standing. Turn your head and left shoulder to the right and take one slow step, encouraging him to follow along with you. Be sure *not* to look back at him. When your dog follows, click and throw the treat forward.

Repeat this until there is no hesitation on his part to move along with you without lagging as you go to the right. Sometimes (about 20 percent of the time) feed by throwing the treat and sometimes (about 80 percent of the time) feed him in position. When you are feeding in position, make sure you feed him so his head is facing forward. This will teach him to keep his body straight. If you feed him to keep him looking at you, you will be teaching him to swing his hind end out. (Hint: You don't want to do this.) He will automatically look back up at you if you have done your homework.

There is some specific footwork for the right turn:

1. Take a small step with your right foot (the length of your foot).
2. Place your left foot at a right angle in front of your right one, so that you are now heel to toe.
3. Make sure your head is pointing to the right, as well as your upper torso.
4. Take a small step with your right foot and then continue heeling with your normal heeling stride.

ABOUT TURN RIGHT

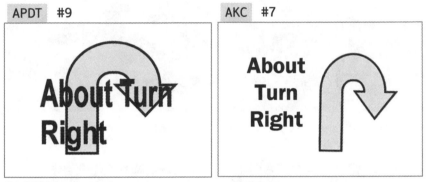

APDT #9   AKC #7

ALL LEVELS   ALL LEVELS

This is very similar to the right turn, except now you are turning in place and going back the way you came. Turn your head to the right and bring your shoulders along with you. Pretend your neck and shoulders are fused together so they move in unison, while you turn your waist.

At the same time, put your left foot in front of your right foot to make a "T."

Bring your right foot up and put your heels together to look like an "L," take a small step with your left foot, and then a regular sized step with your right foot. Continue to bring your entire body around, making sure you don't drag your left shoulder. If you do, you will actually be pushing your dog back, creating a lagging problem.

For those of you who have ever jumped a horse, think of it this way—look to your next jump. For those of you who don't ride, watch where you are driving. It may also be helpful for you to watch your feet as you turn. You will be less likely to drag your head that way and it will help you with your footwork. Be sure you aren't dipping your shoulder down—otherwise it will look like you are a plane that is banking. If you concentrate on pivoting your waist rather than

Correct foot cue as well as shoulder
and head cues for the "T."

Close-up of footwork for the "T."

Correct foot cue as well as shoulder
and head cues for the "L."

Close-up of the "L." Photos: V. Wind.

CHAPTER 3 Basic Maneuvers

Briget's shoulder is dragging and she is looking back at her dog, and so Sempkin is lagging.

bending, you won't fall into "banking the plane." More footwork will be discussed in subsequent chapters but I want you to start training it correctly from the beginning. (Otherwise, you'll have to go back and redo it later—yuck!)

Once you have made the turn slowly and your dog is still with you, click and throw the treat ahead of you. This will teach the dog to whip around you at a brisk pace. Be aware, though, that you don't want to throw the treat ahead to get him to move faster. That will only backfire and teach the dog to lag since that is what you are reinforcing. If your dog is lagging, then move slower, setting him up to stay right next to you. Just like you did with the right turn, feed sometimes in position and sometimes throw the treat ahead of you.

If you find your dog is lagging more often than not, have someone watch you or take a video and see if your left shoulder is too far back or if you are dragging your head to the left in an attempt to keep an eye on your dog. Ninety-nine percent of the time, that is the problem. I call the right turn and about turn the "have faith" turns. Have faith that your dog is there and he will be. You can still see him with your peripheral vision, even with your head turned to the right. If for some reason, because of your body type and/or the size of your dog, you are unable to see him, have faith anyway. Look back at him and guess what? He will be pushed back by your body language and he'll end up lagging.

LEFT TURN

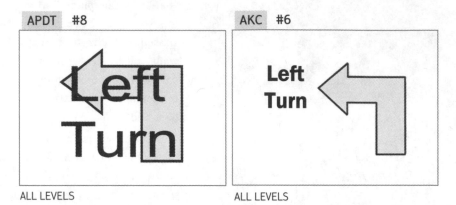

APDT #8

ALL LEVELS

AKC #6

ALL LEVELS

ABOUT U TURN

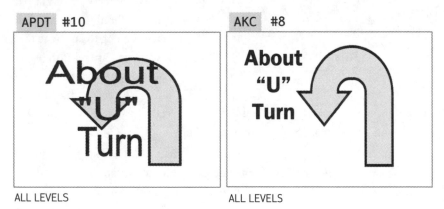

APDT #10

ALL LEVELS

AKC #8

ALL LEVELS

The key to left and about U turns is to teach the dog to move his hind end in as you turn. The best way to start this is to do circles to the left. Begin by doing large left circles and gradually make them smaller and smaller. The behavior you are clicking for here is the hind end moving in. You may have to have someone watch your dog and click for you. Be sure that your body language is correct: your head and shoulders are looking to the left. If your dog is bumping you, push your left shoulder farther back and this should correct the problem. Don't do too many circles in a row because otherwise you will get dizzy. When rewarding for the left circles, place your treat to the left side of your dog's face, so he is actually looking away from you—this will help keep his hind end in.

There are some fun games you can play to help your dog gain hind end awareness. You will be using some props at first but be sure to fade them as quickly as you can. Depending on how quickly *you* catch on (your dog will always catch on faster than you do), you may be able to fade them after a week or so.

"Four Chairs in a Row" Game

This game will not only help with left and U turns, it will also help with any other exercise that has turns—the serpentine, spirals, figure 8, 270 to the left, and 90 degree left and right pivots. Place four chairs in a row, about four to five feet apart. Very slowly, concentrating on your own body posture, walk through the chairs, weaving through them.

Four chairs in a row—Stacey is heeling Codi to the left.

Four broad jump rails in a box—Anna is heeling Po around to the left.

As you are going to the right, make sure your right shoulder is back, your left shoulder is forward and your head is pointing where you are going. Click and treat your dog for staying with you. Then as you go around a chair to the left, make sure your left shoulder is back, your right shoulder is forward and you are watching where you are going. Click and treat your dog for moving his hind end in. The "pressure" of the chair should help him to do this. If your dog is bumping you on the left direction, push your left shoulder back. If he is lagging on the right direction, push your left shoulder forward. Don't forget, don't look back at your dog on the right turns—otherwise you are pushing him back with your posture.

"Four Chairs in a Box" Game

Here is another game you can play to help with hind end awareness. Put the chairs in a box shape. Walk slowly around the chairs, going to the left. As you go around each corner, click and treat your dog for moving his hind end in. Again, watch your own body posture—left shoulder back, right shoulder forward, watch where you are driving. Make sure your dog is not knocking into the chairs—give him a good six inches of room. If you have a toy dog, he might not feel the pressure of the chairs, so you can use broad jump rails placed on edge.

LEFT ABOUT TURNS

APDT #48

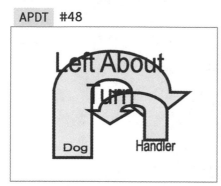

LEVELS 2 & 3

AKC #29

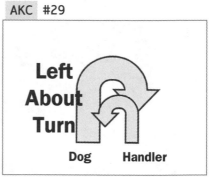

Dog   Handler

ALL LEVELS

This is commonly called the "Schutzhund about turn," primarily because this is the about turn used in the sport of Schutzund. The left about turn looks really hard, but in fact is very easy to train and fun to do. I like to teach it in the beginning during Rally 1 classes for just that reason. The prerequisite for doing the left about is to make sure your dog knows the right finish. You walk slowly, turn in to the dog (staying in place), giving your "around" (right finish) cue (either verbal or with your right hand signal) at the same time. Then stand still for a second and wait for your dog's nose to appear on your left. Once you see his nose, click and throw the treat ahead of you. Don't throw the treat to *get* your dog to be in heel position— click and throw the treat ahead of you *because* he is in heel position. As with the right about turn, feed sometimes in heel position and sometimes throw the treat ahead of you.

In APDT Rally, this exercise only appears in levels 2 and 3, so you don't have to worry about handling the leash.

Jane is turning in to Ruby while giving the "around" hand signal cue.

To further reinforce the forward movement, Jane is now tossing the treat ahead because Ruby has caught up with her.

In AKC Rally, however, the exercise may be in Novice (on leash). To handle the leash for this, before you give your around signal, put the leash in your right hand. Then give your signal. As you are turning in to your dog and he goes around you, reach behind you and pick up the leash with your left hand.

THE DANCE (A.K.A. HEELING)

Many people think that competition-style heeling looks very militaristic. I look at it as a beautiful dance. Before we get into more of the behaviors needed to complete each sign, you and your dog need to know how to heel.

My favorite way to teach heeling is off leash in a safe area or on a long, dragging, fifty-foot line. It is better to give the dog the choice to be glued to your leg and then reinforce that choice, rather than force the dog into position. We all learn better when something is presented in a fun and rewarding way.

At this point, your dog should be having fun doing all of these stationary exercises and you are most likely getting rapt attention. If you aren't, go back to Chapter 2 and review the exercises there before moving onto heeling.

You will begin your heeling lessons by walking briskly, left arm on your stomach, elbow tucked in, head and shoulders straight. You want to start this training by showing your dog the "right" picture. Don't say anything, just start walking.

The instant your dog comes anywhere near heel position, click and treat and then change direction. Repeat this exercise for a few minutes at a time in many different locations (again, no Rally trials will be held in your backyard) for about one to two weeks. Mix in the "tag, you're it" game (see Chapter 2) and run around and be silly. Once your dog is staying with you and you couldn't get rid of him even if you tried, you may go onto the next step.

As with any exercise in this book, make sure you don't name the behavior in the beginning stages, because your dog doesn't know it yet. Name it when it is perfect.

Now you should start walking in straight lines with a few turns to keep it interesting for both you and your dog. As you are turning, say your dog's name and "this way" in a happy voice. Be sure that you are also concentrating on your own head and shoulder cues when you turn. Add in some speed changes— move slowly, speed up and then jog. Go back to some turns and then straight lines—mix it up to keep it fun. Gradually make the lines longer and longer. You are also going to be more picky about when you click and how you feed:

- *When*: Your dog is in more perfect heel position—not lagging, forging, too wide or bumping your leg.
- *When*: Your dog is looking up at your face. Be sure your face and shoulders are pointing forward. You can still look down (toward your feet—keeping your head straight) and make eye contact with your dog out of the corner of your eye.
- *How*: You are going to feed so his head is straight. Don't worry, he will look back up at you. If you feed him with his head up, his hind end will crab out.

You also need to start being consistent with your footwork. Heeling should be different than just plain walking: your footwork is a cue to your dog that you are now heeling rather than just out for a walk, and it looks smoother and more "professional."

When heeling, you stand up straighter and lean ever so slightly forward at the waist. You start on the heel of your foot, roll on your foot to your toes, and then push off on your toes for the next step. Keep the length of your stride the same each time once you have adjusted it according to the size of your dog. You don't want to be taking very large strides if you have a toy dog or short strides if you have a giant breed dog. (See Chapter 4 for help in establishing the "normal" pace for you and your dog.) If it helps to keep your stride the same for each step, you may rub your knees/legs together as you walk—not enough to look ridiculous, just enough to stay constant. This is also useful for turns. Otherwise you may have a tendency to walk into your dog, thus pushing him out or tripping on your own feet.

Heeling really isn't much more complicated than that. The hard part about heeling is getting it perfect at a trial among all the different distractions. That is why you are going to practice this absolutely everywhere —parking lots, shopping centers, parks, trails, city streets—whatever location you can think up. Gather a few friends and train together. The harder the distractions, the more reinforcing you need to be. Some of the many things you can use as reinforcers are listed in Chapter 2.

In his book *Clicker Training for Obedience*, Morgan Spector presents a wonderful chart that he follows to build stamina (both mental and physical) and really great heeling. If you use this chart, it will also help you to be more variable in

Walking normally—note the body posture and the space between the legs.

Heeling—now can you see the difference? Photos: V. Wind.

CHAPTER 3 Basic Maneuvers

when you reinforce, so you don't get stuck reinforcing after the same number of steps each time. We humans are creatures of habit and tend to stay in a rut of reinforcement patterns. This can cause problems (see Chapter 8), so work to be unpredictable.

While Mr. Spector's book is geared for competition obedience, heeling is a big part of Rally. In fact, you will be doing more heeling (that is, heeling for longer periods of time) in Rally than you would in competition obedience.

LEVEL 1 (mean* = 5 steps): 5 steps, 2, 6, 3, 7, 3, 5, 1, 7, 4, 3, 5, 1 (52 steps)

LEVEL 2 (7 steps): 7 steps, 3, 10, 5, 8, 4, 7, 2, 5, 10, 3, 7, 2 (73 steps)

LEVEL 3 (10 steps): 10 steps, 5, 8, 4, 12, 6, 10, 3, 7, 10, 5, 12, 1, 10, 3 (106 steps)

LEVEL 4 (12 steps): 12, 6, 10, 4, 15, 7, 12, 6, 15, 8, 12, 2, 10, 4 (123 steps)

LEVEL 5 (15 steps): 15, 7, 12, 8, 13, 6, 20, 2, 10, 7, 15, 9, 20, 12, 8, 15, 7, 3 (189 steps)

LEVEL 6 (20 steps): 20, 10, 12, 8, 15, 9, 17, 10, 25, 15, 3, 20, 10, 25, 13, 5 (217 steps)

LEVEL 7 (25 steps): 15, 25, 12, 20, 5, 15, 25, 2, 18, 30, 12, 25, 15, 20, 25, 12, 3 (279 steps)

LEVEL 8 (30 steps): 25, 30, 15, 20, 10, 17, 35, 5, 25, 30, 15, 20, 35, 17, 30, 15, 5 (349 steps)

*Mean *indicates, for each level, the number of steps that occurs most frequently. You can see that the mean gradually increases from level to level, as does the total number of steps.*

Count your steps and click and treat at each one of those numbers. In the beginning, it may be useful if you have someone counting your steps and clicking for you. This is one of the very few times when you need not worry about precision—especially in the beginning. For instance, at level 1, just click and treat your dog even if he isn't in perfect heel position. Once you get to the end of that row and go on to level 2, you will see your dog become glued to your leg. Don't worry about turns right now; just do some nice straight lines or heel in a big oval.

As Mr. Spector says, "You are getting substantial increases in the amount of heeling done from one level to the next, but *to the dog* it does not seem so bad because it is in 'doses' measured by the VR (variable reinforcement) schedule."

If at any time you find your dog wandering off, take a look at the level you are working on—perhaps it is too much for him. This chart is not the be-all and end-all—feel free to adjust it depending on your own dog. Just back down a few steps and go on from there. Be careful that you aren't drilling, drilling, drilling your dog. Make it fun for the two of you; add in some play as well. For instance, in the middle of some heeling, run around and play or toss toys for a minute or so, and then go back into your heeling pattern. Add in some surprise elements in terms of new and different types of reinforcers and you won't be able to lose your dog!

RALLY AROUND

* Keep your sessions short and fun and be sure to use many different types of reinforcers.
* Do only a few repetitions of each behavior so that it remains fun for you and your dog.
* Be sure to add in lots of play and surprise reinforcers.
* Practice in many different locations.

◄ 4 ►

RED LIGHT, GREEN LIGHT

In the last chapter, among other things, you learned how to teach the heel. Because so many of the remaining signs have a halt in them, it is now important that you learn how to stop. However, before you teach your dog to stop when you do, you need to know the proper footwork. This is an important cue to your dog that you are, in fact, going to stop really soon. If you just stop short, your dog will keep going. Getting a stop and an automatic sit is very important for quite a few of the behaviors needed for both AKC and APDT Rally.

HALT AND AUTOMATIC SIT

Practice this first without your dog:

1. Take one small step (the length of your foot—not an entire stride) with your left foot.
2. Take one small step with your right foot.
3. Bring your left foot up to meet your right foot.

You may chant to yourself, "left, right, stop." If your toes are all thumbs like mine are, believe me, it will help. Feel free to look down at your toes when practicing this. It will help you later on when you do it with your dog. You can still see your dog if you are looking at your feet.

Once you can do this without thinking about it, add in pretend heeling before you stop. Continue to practice until you can make a smooth transition. Be sure you don't slow down while you are stopping; just do your footwork and stop. When you are comfortable, you can put your dog into the picture. You will "back chain" the halt for him:

"Come up" using a lure—note Stacey's hand position. It is slightly in to lure Codi's head closer to her.

Luring the dog into a sit—again note Stacey's hand position. It is now above Codi's head.

1. Stand with your dog in heel position.
2. Take a small step with your *right* foot.
3. At the same time, say "come up," and lure your dog forward with you.
4. As you bring your left foot to be next to your right foot, raise your hand up to lure him into a straight sit.

Remember back chaining? This is where you train the last part of a behavior first. In this case, the halt consists of left/right/stop. So we are going to train the last part first—the right/stop. When you put it all together, your dog will have record-speed sits every time you stop and the crowd will ooh and aah.

Be sure to keep your hand in front of your dog's nose to keep his body straight. Practice in front of a mirror so you can see, without twisting your body, if in fact your dog is straight. Click and treat for all straight sits. If your dog is sitting crooked more often than not, that only means your lure is off. If your dog

has a tendency to sit with his hind end out, place your hand so you are feeding him with his head turned away from you. As an added benefit, your dog will be doing what is commonly called a tuck sit rather than a rock back sit. (A *tuck sit* is when the dog's hind end comes forward into his front feet. This is the preferred sit for competition, because his head remains in heel position. A *rock back sit* is when the dog's front feet move back into his hind feet. If your dog does this sit, he will be behind you when you halt and will no longer be in heel position.)

Anna is luring Belle to do a come up/sit using a target stick.

Tuck sit—note how the "dog" remains in heel position and her "front feet" are close to her back feet. Photos: J. Crow.

Rock back sit—note that the "dog" is now no longer in heel position and her back feet are farther away from her front feet.

Because Codi is a larger, less supple dog, he needs a more forward lure to get into heel position.

If your dog's hind end goes out, don't get fooled into thinking you should push it in with your hand. This will only make him resist and he will move even farther away because of the pressure.

It is very easy to teach a tuck sit without any physical manipulation. Just grab some string cheese—don't cut it up into tiny pieces. Do the same luring into the sit in heel and front positions, but let your dog nibble the cheese as you bring his head up very high (not so high that he has to jump for it). Because his head will be high, his hind end will naturally scoot forward into his front legs. I like to use string cheese because it is harder for a dog to bite off a chunk than when I use a hotdog. Once he has scooted, lower your hand slightly and click him for sitting.

If your dog is very hairy or very small, or if you can't quite see if he is tucking, have someone help you click when he has done the tuck. Bigger dogs may have a problem with this depending on their conformation. Try not to get frustrated—just keep going. If you have to, bring your hand a little farther forward when doing the tuck in heel position.

As I mentioned earlier, I use lures sparingly. Most of the time, they become the actual hand signal. However, in the case of the automatic sit, use the hand lure longer than for any other behavior to make sure the dog is moving with you and sitting perfectly straight. The caveat with using a lure is that it really must be faded out as quickly as possible. I mention in the above text a few weeks of using the lure. If your dog catches on faster, then by all means fade the lure faster, or use it sparingly.

In the beginning, you will have actually four cues for the automatic sit:

* Your footwork
* Your lure hand
* The words "come up"
* The word "sit"

Don't be alarmed—you will be fading all but the first cue very quickly. For the first week or two, practice this from a standstill; come up/sit, come up/sit, come up/sit, using all four cues. Be sure to click and treat each time your dog does it correctly. Make it into a fun game—do about five to six repetitions at a time and then add in some play. If you make it too tedious, both you and your dog will lose interest. At about the second-week mark, fade out your hand signal (by making it smaller and smaller) and just use your footwork and the verbal "come up" and "sit." At the third week, fade out all verbal cues (by saying them softer and softer) and just use your foot cues. If at any time your dog doesn't do it correctly, go back to a small lure a few times and then fade it again once he remembers.

If you find your dog is forging, do your hand motion sooner—as soon as your left foot is coming up to meet with your right foot.

Now you will pat your head and rub your stomach—in other words, put heeling together with an automatic sit. Move slowly at first—not really for your dog but for yourself. Don't forget to chant to yourself, "left, right, stop." The funny thing is that once you have a dog by your side, all of a sudden the tendency is to forget your footwork. Heel a few steps and halt when you are ready. Try not to hesitate during this process—keep your pace the same. If you need to lure a bit the first few times, that's okay.

Once you can heel for a few steps and halt—you with the proper footwork cues and your dog responding with the proper behavior (straight, fast, tuck sit), you are ready to move on to some new Rally signs.

STOP AND GO

HALT/SIT

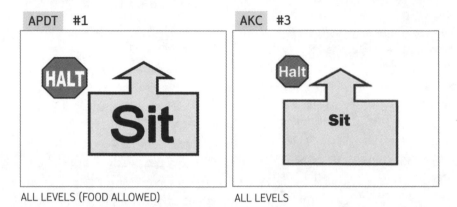

APDT #1

ALL LEVELS (FOOD ALLOWED)

AKC #3

ALL LEVELS

See! What did I tell you! You already know this sign!

HALT/SIT/STAND

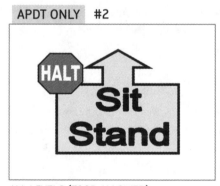

APDT ONLY #2

ALL LEVELS (FOOD ALLOWED)

You are halfway to completing this sign. You have the automatic sit and now you are just going to add in the stand. (See Chapter 3 for instructions on teaching the stand.) You halt, your dog sits automatically, and then you give your hand signal to stand. Then you'll be moving on to the next sign! Piece of cake!

Quigley is now standing, and Andrea will heel off from there.

HALT/STAND/SIT

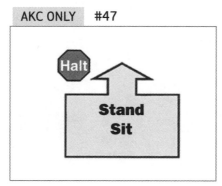

AKC ONLY   #47

Halt

Stand
Sit

EXCELLENT LEVEL

This is almost identical to the sign above, except that after your dog halts along with you and automatically sits, you will ask him to stand, then sit again, and then continue heeling.

HALT/STAND/DOWN

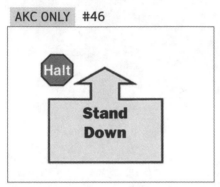

AKC ONLY   #46

Stand
Down

EXCELLENT LEVEL

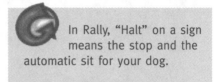

In Rally, "Halt" on a sign means the stop and the automatic sit for your dog.

Very simply, halt (your dog automatically sits), stand your dog, down him, and then continue heeling without a sit. No sit is allowed between the stand and the down.

HALT/SIT/DOWN/SIT

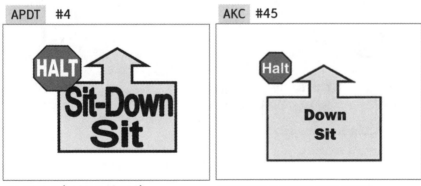

APDT   #4

Sit-Down
Sit

ALL LEVELS (FOOD ALLOWED)

AKC   #45

Down
Sit

ADVANCED & EXCELLENT LEVELS

These two signs are really the same, and again they are easy! Yippee! Halt, your dog sits; you ask him to down and then sit again, and off you go!

HALT/SIT/DOWN

APDT #3

HALT **Sit** **Down**

ALL LEVELS (FOOD ALLOWED)

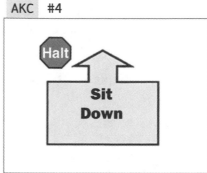

AKC #4

Halt **Sit Down**

ALL LEVELS

This sign is pretty self-explanatory. You halt, your dog sits, you ask for a down and then you move on to the next sign. You want your dog to down next to you, not in front of you. When you are training this, use your left hand to lure him into the down. If you use your right hand, he will have an inclination to lie down in front of you to get closer to your treat hand.

Andrea using her left hand to signal Flute for the down.

Andrea leaning slightly forward, saying "heel" but waiting for Quigley to get up before proceeding.

To make this exercise flow better, once you are ready to continue, say your heel word, hesitate for a second so your dog has a chance to get up, and then heel on. You want your leash to be loose and you want to look like a team, so if you rush to the next station, your dog will be left in the dust—not pretty.

HALT/SIT/WALK AROUND

APDT #5

ALL LEVELS (FOOD ALLOWED)

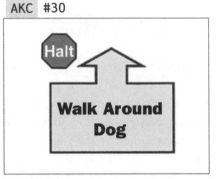

AKC #30

ALL LEVELS

This exercise is a little harder because you have to teach the dog to sit and stay while you walk around. You halt, your dog sits, he stays, and you walk around him and come back to heel position. The leash adds a small complication.

Practice this without the leash first. Ask your dog to sit. Hold a treat over his head (you can let him nibble) while you walk around him from the front. Click and treat when you are back to heel position. Be sure your hand stays steady over his nose—if you don't, he'll shift around as though on a Lazy Susan as he follows your hand. Repeat this about a dozen times (not all in a row—we are not drilling here), and fade your hand over his head so you will be able to just walk around him without using it. If your dog already has a solid stay

Be sure to have a loose leash. Both AKC and APDT take off many points for a tight leash. Most of the time this is handler error, often due to the handler being in a rush to get to the next sign, forgetting completely about the poor dog attached to the other end of the leash. Keep your eyes on your dog, and don't forget that he is the other half of your team.

Andrea walking around Darcy, letting her nibble on a treat.

Andrea walking around Darcy, now with a leash on. Note that the leash is held high so it doesn't wrap around Darcy's neck.

(see the honor exercise in Chapter 7) while you return to heel position, this is very easy.

Once you and your dog can do this off leash, add the leash. Ask your dog to stay. Keep the leash in your left hand and hold it loosely so you don't inadvertently tug on it (which will then encourage him to move). You may also hold it high so it doesn't wrap around his neck.

HALT/SIT/DOWN/WALK AROUND

APDT #6

ALL LEVELS (FOOD ALLOWED)

AKC #31

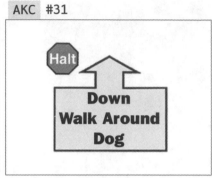

ALL LEVELS

This exercise is very similar to the one above. You halt, your dog sits, and you ask him to down and stay. You walk around him from the front and go back to heel position, and then off the two of you go to the next sign. Don't forget that, because he is lying down, you must give your dog a second to get up. That way the leash won't be tight and he won't lag. Say your heel word, count to one, and then continue heeling.

Andrea walking around Darcy in a down with a leash on. Again, note that the leash is held high so it doesn't wrap around Darcy's neck.

HALT/STAND/WALK AROUND DOG

#36

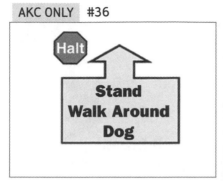

ADVANCED & EXCELLENT LEVELS

Even though this particular sign is only in AKC, you will need to train it for similar signs in APDT, so don't skip this exercise even if you plan on doing only APDT. Once he is sitting after the halt, stand your dog, tell him to stay and walk around him. Go around him from the front (as you

Andrea walking around Darcy while she is standing.

do in the other walk around exercises) and continue so you end up back in heel position. Then move on to the next exercise.

You train this the same way as you did the others. Depending on the size of your dog, it may be a bit harder to keep his head straight while you walk around. Break it down into tiny pieces:

1. Stand your dog and ask him to stay. Take one step as if to go around, click him if he doesn't move, and reach your hand back to give him a treat while his head is still pointing forward.

2. Take another step, click, and reach back to give him a treat.

3. Repeat until you have gone all the way around.

To fade all of the treats, now take two steps, click and treat, then three steps, and so on. If you have a huge dog, you may have to use a helper to deliver the treats for you in the beginning. If at any time your dog moves, just stand still, count to three, and start over.

HALT/1, 2, 3 STEPS FORWARD

APDT #27

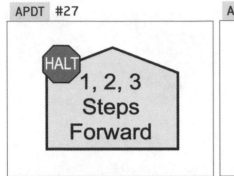

ALL LEVELS
(FOOD ALLOWED AFTER THE FINISH)

AKC #25

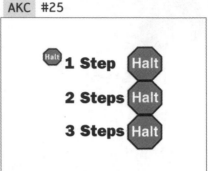

ALL LEVELS

When I first saw this sign, I said *"What???"* It is really quite simple, however, as long as you have been practicing your automatic sits.

Halt: You approach the sign and halt. Your dog automatically sits.

1 step: Take a small step with your right foot, and bring your left foot up to meet your right one, asking your dog to come up/sit as you take that second step.

2 steps: Ask your dog to come up/sit as you take a small step with your left foot; then take a small step with your right foot, and as you bring your left foot up to meet your right foot, ask your dog again to come up/sit.

3 steps: As you step off on your right foot, tell your dog to come up/sit; then step with your left foot, then your right one, and as your left foot comes up to meet your right foot, ask your dog to come up/sit.

This particular sign has a few caveats:

➡ Don't use your heel word for the 1-2-3 steps. Heel means to "move 'em out" and we want your dog to stay with you. Use your "come up/sit" as your verbal cue and your dog will remain close by and not forge ahead.

➡ Both APDT and AKC Rally allow you to talk during your run. So that you won't make a mistake in counting the number of steps needed, please do count out loud to yourself. It would be too bad to get a non-qualify or to get major points taken off because of something as silly as not taking the correct number of steps. (Been there, done that!)

➡ Be sure to make each of the 1-2-3 steps small—the length of your foot, rather than your normal heeling stride. These little steps become extra cues for your dog that will make it very clear you will be stopping.

➡ If you are using food in APDT, you can only use it *after* the three steps are complete and only *before* you move forward to the next sign.

CALL FRONT/1, 2, 3 STEPS BACKWARD

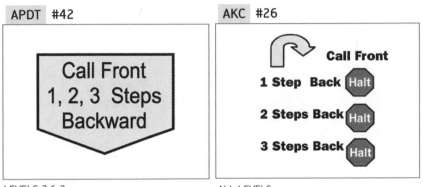

APDT #42

Call Front
1, 2, 3 Steps
Backward

AKC #26

Call Front

1 Step Back Halt

2 Steps Back Halt

3 Steps Back Halt

LEVELS 2 & 3
(FOOD ALLOWED AFTER THE FINISH)

ALL LEVELS

I like this sign a lot because it lets you change direction from the forward movement of most of the other signs. You are heeling and you call your dog to you as you back up in the direction you just came from (three steps maximum depending on the size of your dog). Your dog sits straight in front of you. You back up one step and encourage your dog to follow and stop as you stop. Your dog sits straight in front of you. Then take two steps backward and encourage your dog to follow you. Again, have him sit front as you stop. Now take three steps backward and encourage your dog to follow and end with a sit front as you stop. Because you are both no longer headed in the same direction, there will be another sign next to this one to tell you which finish to do—the right or left finish. Don't forget—if the finish asked for is a left finish and you are doing this exercise on leash, you can keep the leash in your left hand. If it is the right finish, switch the leash to your right hand before giving your around cue.

You may count out loud in this exercise as well: "one, come/sit," "one, two, come/sit" and "one, two, three, come/sit." Say your come word *as* you move backward. You don't need any special footwork for this exercise—one less thing to worry about. If competing on leash, when you call your dog to front position be sure not to yank on the leash. Say your dog's name, take the first backward step, and then say "come." Pretty soon the two of you will be moving like a well-oiled machine.

MOVING DOWN & FORWARD

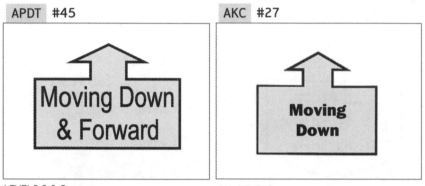

APDT #45

Moving Down & Forward

LEVELS 2 & 3

AKC #27

Moving Down

ALL LEVELS

This is a fun behavior and not hard at all. Yes, maybe my Border Collies and Sheltie make it easy for me, but most of my students have nontraditional obedience breeds (Bull Mastiffs, English Mastiffs, Daschunds, Rottweilers, Greater Swiss Mountain Dogs, Bull Terriers, Collies, Beagles, Bassett Bleus, Papillons and a wide variety of mixed breeds and body types), and all of them can do the moving down with speed and alacrity.

As you approach this sign, ask your dog to down—no sit is allowed here; the dog must do a down from the standing/heeling position. You will then wait for a count of two and ask your dog to heel. Say your heel word, count to one and once your dog gets up, continue heeling.

Just as there are two kinds of sits (the rock back and tuck), there are two kinds of downs—the sphinx down and the "on a hip" down. For this exercise, the sphinx down is preferable (but not required), since it will allow your dog to get down and back up more quickly. If your dog's body type doesn't allow for the sphinx down, or if he physically can't (perhaps because of arthritis or hip problems), don't sweat it.

To simplify this behavior for your dog, train the sphinx down without heeling at first. Do this when your dog is standing—place your hand with a treat in front of your dog's nose. Slowly bring the treat down to the ground and slightly

Andrea signaling Flute into the moving down.

in toward his chest. This will help him to lean back slightly and, most likely, he will do the down properly. If he tries to sit first, release him and just try again. When he gets it right, be sure to click and jackpot the first few attempts. This will help cement in his brain that this behavior is a good thing.

Once your dog is doing the down in front of you, practice the same thing with him next to you. Be sure to use your left hand—otherwise he may try to get in front of you. Fade out your hand signal and get the down on a verbal cue. (Remember, you don't *have* to fade out hand cues for Rally, since you can use verbal and hand signals in either venue.)

When your dog has mastered the sphinx down, add in heeling to get the "moving down" part. Heel slowly at first and ask or lure your dog into the down position. As your proficiency level increases, speed up your heeling to your normal pace. Make it a fun game for your dog to "down" like a Border Collie! Just as with the come up/sits, when training the moving down, too much repetition will turn you both off. Just do a few fast downs and then run around, act silly, and go on to something else.

Even though this sign says "moving down," you do have to stop for a brief second; otherwise, your dog will be lagging.

BONUS EXERCISE: MOVING DOWN/LEAVE DOG CALL FRONT/FINISH RIGHT OR LEFT

APDT ONLY

LEVEL 2

This is a bonus exercise and is performed *after* you have completed your run and crossed the finish line. You are not required to do the exercise. However, you must let the judge know before you begin your run whether or not you will be performing it, and then you are committed to that choice. The bonus exercise time is not included in your course time.

After crossing the finish line, you heel to the bonus exercise sign "Moving Down, Leave Dog." When you get to the sign, you cue your dog to down. Without hesitating (as you would on the above exercise), you leave your dog and move to the next bonus exercise sign, "Turn, Call Front/Finish R/L." At this sign, you turn, face the dog and call him to front. Your dog must come promptly to the front position. You then cue him to finish either right or left. The exercise is complete once your dog is sitting in heel position after the finish.

The training of this exercise is really quite simple. Once you have the moving down in the previous exercise, just practice it without the hesitation and signal your dog to stay as you walk away.

YOU ARE AMBIDEXTROUS

CALL FRONT/FORWARD RIGHT

APDT #15

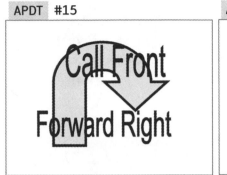

ALL LEVELS

AKC #13

ALL LEVELS

CALL FRONT/FINISH RIGHT

APDT #17

ALL LEVELS
(FOOD ALLOWED AFTER FINISH)

AKC #15

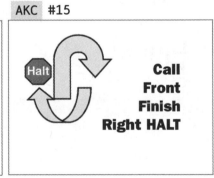

ALL LEVELS

CALL FRONT/FORWARD LEFT

APDT #16

ALL LEVELS

AKC #14

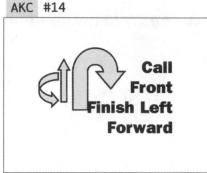

ALL LEVELS

CALL FRONT/FINISH LEFT

APDT #18

ALL LEVELS
(FOOD ALLOWED AFTER FINISH)

AKC #16

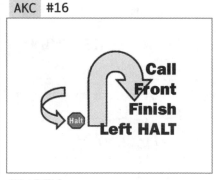

ALL LEVELS

I am grouping these four signs together because they are very similar. The "call front" is the same for each sign. You are heeling, you say your dog's name and back up a step or two (no more than three steps are allowed). Your dog follows you and sits front (I know it doesn't say to sit front—this is something you'll just have to remember).

You will see below that I have divided the "forward" exercises into APDT and AKC. They have slightly different handling "rules."

Forward Right

- *APDT*—You have your dog do the right finish, but once he is heel position and before he sits, you continue heeling.
- *AKC*—Same as above, except you start heeling as you signal your dog to do the right finish.

Forward Left

- *APDT*—You ask your dog to do the left finish and, again, as soon as he reaches heel position, you continue heeling.
- *AKC*—Same as above, except you start heeling as you signal your dog to do the left finish.

Finish Left

- *APDT and AKC*—You do a left finish, and your dog ends up sitting in heel position.

Finish Right

- *APDT and AKC*—You do the right finish, and your dog ends up sitting in heel position.

Molly calling Tuffy to front position.

If you just think about it this way, you shouldn't have any problems remembering which is which: "Finish" means the dog sits in heel position and "forward" means you move forward—no sit. The words "right" and "left" indicate which direction you cue your dog to go in.

For the left finish or forward, continue to keep the leash in your left hand. For the right finish or forward, you will have to switch the leash to your right hand, give your hand signal and then pick it up with your left hand, just like you did when you practiced the finishes (Chapter 3).

CALL FRONT/ABOUT TURN/FORWARD

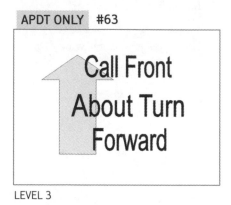

APDT ONLY #63

Call Front
About Turn
Forward

LEVEL 3

This exercise is similar to the above ones because there is a call front. Once your dog is sitting in front of you, you will do your about turn footwork and cue your dog to move along with you in heel position. You then proceed to the next station. You have the choice of turning either to your right (about turn) or to the left (about U turn).

HALT/CALL DOG FRONT/FINISH RIGHT/LEFT AND FORWARD

AKC ONLY #41

Halt
Halt

**Call Dog Front
Finish Right**

ADVANCED & EXCELLENT LEVELS

AKC ONLY #42

Halt
Halt

**Call Dog Front
Finish Left**

ADVANCED & EXCELLENT LEVELS

These signs are similar to the ones above but do have important differences. You heel and then halt. Your dog sits. You then, *without taking any steps backward to aid your dog*, call your dog to front position. Then do the type of finish listed on the sign.

There are a few different ways you can train this:

➤ You can lure the dog to front position from the heel. Depending on the size of your dog, you may need to take one step backward to start and then fade that step.

- You can lure the dog to front as in the previous option and then toss the treat between your legs. This will help your dog to move quickly and to move to perfect front position.

- When you are playing the "front" game (Chapter 2)—once your dog is proficient at it—stand so that you are facing off to one side, so that he has to find the front position. Start this so you are only mildly crooked, and then very crooked. Click and treat all straight fronts.

Andrea is standing crooked as she is about to call Flute to her.

Flute is starting to adjust herself to come in straight...

...and Andrea spreads her legs and tosses a treat to further reinforce the straight front.

BONUS EXERCISE: CALL FRONT/SIDE STEP R/L

APDT ONLY

BONUS

Call Front
Sidestep R/L

LEVEL 1

This new bonus sign is a little tricky. You heel up to the sign, back up a few steps and call your dog front. Your dog sits and you then step either to the right or left, your dog comes with you and sits again in a perfect straight front. There is no finish to this exercise.

You are allowed to use a hand signal (not a lure) for this, but I prefer to train it with just a verbal come cue. In the previous exercise (AKC – Call Dog Front/Finish right or left), you have been working on tossing the treat in between your legs and having your dog follow the treat to build on your straight fronts from an angle. Continue to do so and you should start to see your dog coming in straighter and straighter. Use your eyes and keep your shoulders straight to help guide him in. If he is really looking at you, this will help a great deal.

Every dog seems to be either right or left-handed just as we are, so practice in both directions to see which way he does better.

BONUS EXERCISE: HALT/LEAVE DOG/
TURN CALL TO FRONT (ANGLED)/FINISH R/L

APDT ONLY #32

HALT

Halt
Leave Dog

LEVEL 2

APDT ONLY #33

Turn
Call to Front
(angled)
Finish R/L

LEVEL 2

This new level 2 sign is actually very similar to the Call Front/Side Step R/L in that the dog has to find front. You will leave your dog at the Halt Leave Dog sign and your dog sits in heel position. Ask your dog to stay and you will go to the 2nd sign, which is 15-20 feet away and turn to face the direction of your dog but not directly facing your dog. You will turn and face your dog, but not really face your dog. For instance, he will be facing due North and you will be facing due South, but you will be on a different plane — usually about four to six feet off center. You will train this the same way as you did the above exercise. Because you have more room for the recall part, just use your eyes and head to help guide him in—not your shoulders. Be sure to give your dog enough room to finish so he doesn't knock over the sign.

This is where you'll be standing—off center to where your dog is sitting.

CHANGING LANES

FAST PACE

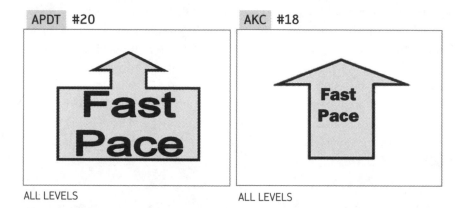

APDT #20

ALL LEVELS

AKC #18

ALL LEVELS

SLOW PACE

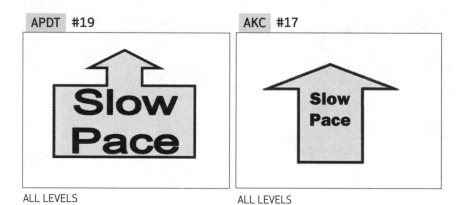

APDT #19

ALL LEVELS

AKC #17

ALL LEVELS

NORMAL PACE

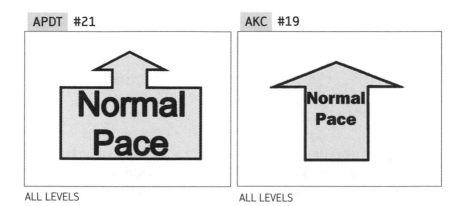

APDT #21

Normal Pace

ALL LEVELS

AKC #19

Normal Pace

ALL LEVELS

These exercises are almost self-explanatory. *Fast* means that you jog at such a speed that your dog (depending on his size) either runs along with you or at least trots at a very fast pace. If you have a tiny dog, this does not mean you should leave him in the dust—this isn't a foot race. *Slow* means that you want to go slowly enough that your dog is walking. *Normal* is when your dog is trotting comfortably. The judge wants to see very specific changes of pace (walk/trot/canter—or at least a very fast trot in place of the canter) and doesn't want to have to guess if you are doing a pace correctly. If you have to leave 'em guessing, I can pretty much guarantee that the decision won't go in your favor.

You need to make sure your normal pace is consistent throughout your performance. Everyone has different length legs and different size dogs. To determine if your normal pace is the correct one for your dog, you need a metronome and a helper. Start with these three different base points:

- → I am five feet tall, and my dogs are twenty inches tall. I set the metronome for 136 beats per minute (BPM).
- → One of my students is about five feet six inches tall, and her dog is about ten inches tall. Her metronome setting is 120 BPM.
- → Another student is five feet tall, and her dog is twenty-eight inches tall. Her setting is 145 BPM.

Each beat is a footfall. You may want to practice heeling to the metronome first without your dog. Make sure you are rolling your feet, standing in the correct posture and that your stride is the same with each beat. Once you are comfortable with pairing the sound of the metronome with each footfall, add in your dog. (Don't skip this step! You will need it at a later date.)

Based on the previous examples, you may want to set the metronome at, say, 130 beats per minute and go up or down from there. You need to have someone watching to see if your dog is trotting comfortably, that is, not too slow and not too fast—just right. Raise or lower the beats per minute as needed. Then continue to practice with the metronome until you are very consistent with the pace you have now established as normal.

For your slow pace, you can make your stride a little smaller and you can stand up a little straighter (I also breathe slower). For the fast, a somewhat longer stride with your torso tilted a bit forward is fine. No matter the pace, you should still be doing the heel/center/toe roll with your feet, and your body posture should be mostly upright with your left hand up at your waist, elbow tucked in.

SMOOTH TRANSITIONS

To make the entire routine look smooth and more "professional," and to give your dog the proper cues, smooth transitions between pace changes are very important. I make it my goal to do three paces to gear up or slow down between each pace change. That way your dog isn't forging or sitting when you slow down or lagging when you speed up. For instance, if you slow down and your dog sits, you need to make sure you didn't push your torso too far back and that you eased into the slow.

RALLY AROUND

- Some of the exercises in this chapter may seem tedious—keep them fun for you and your dog by adding in lots of play.
- Make sure that while doing all of your turns, your pace remains the same. Practice a lot with the metronome and it will become second nature for you.
- If your dog is having problems with these behaviors due to footwork issues on your own part, go back to working without your dog until you get it right.

---

chapter

5

IN AND OUT, BACK AND FORTH

Most of the turns you will encounter in Rally are given in this chapter. For those of you who have also shown in competition obedience, many of these will be very familiar. For those of you who haven't yet competed, not to worry—they are quite easy to learn and fun to teach.

OOPS! WHERE DID YOU GO?

SPIRAL RIGHT/DOG OUTSIDE

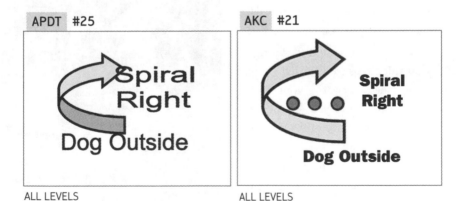

APDT #25	AKC #21
Spiral Right Dog Outside	Spiral Right Dog Outside
ALL LEVELS	ALL LEVELS

Prepare to get dizzy with the signs above and on the next page! Your foot and shoulder work will come in handy here. Your dog should stay right with you, rather than bumping your leg or going wide. Three cones are set up in a line, five

SPIRAL LEFT/DOG INSIDE

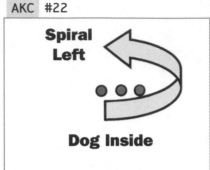

ALL LEVELS   ALL LEVELS

feet apart (in AKC they are anywhere from six to eight feet apart). You'll heel around the cones so that your dog is either on the inside or outside. At first you'll heel around all three cones in a big circle, then two cones in one complete circle and then one cone in a complete circle. I find it very easy to become disoriented and forget how many cones I've gone around, so I recommend that you count, either out loud or to yourself, "Three, two, one" as you go around.

When you go around to the right (dog outside), be sure your left shoulder is pushed forward, your right shoulder is back and you are looking away from your dog toward the direction you are moving.

If you are moving to the right but looking back at your dog, your dog will lag. When you go around the cones with your dog on the inside, be sure to push your left shoulder back and right shoulder forward.

I am heeling around the spiral to the left with Beau on the inside, closer to the cones. Photo: A. Kelly.

I am heeling around the spiral to the right with Beau on the outside, farther from the cones. Photo: A. Kelly.

As you move around the ends of the spiral, make sure your shoulder and head cues are in place. As you come to a straightaway, square up your body cues so that your dog stays in heel position and doesn't continue to wrap around.

Be sure to practice the "four chairs in a row" game (see Chapter 3) so you and your dog are comfortable—you in giving the correct body cues and your dog in following those cues correctly.

MOVING SIDE STEP RIGHT

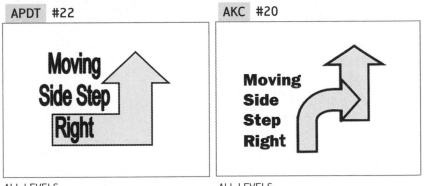

APDT #22

Moving Side Step Right

ALL LEVELS

AKC #20

Moving Side Step Right

ALL LEVELS

This exercise is fun to teach but may be a little challenging. The finished product will look like this: You heel in a straight line, take a big step to the right, your dog staying with you as you move, and then continue (without stopping) to move forward in a straight line.

The added benefit of teaching this is that if you need to adjust your position on the start line, you can just move to the right and your dog will follow. This way, you won't have to heel around in a circle to get to where you should have been. In real life, you can bypass anything unpleasant on the road or trail or move away from another dog that you are uncomfortable with and your dog will come with you.

You train this exercise in small approximations (steps).

"Lean to the Right" Game

Have your dog in heel position—standing is best. Lean to the right as you pat your leg to encourage him to lean in to you. Click and treat for any movement toward you. Don't worry about him staying in position or staying straight—you just want him to move with you at this stage. You can however, feed him with his head straight, as this will help you later on.

"Fade to the Right" Game

Once your dog is leaning along with you, you can move on to this step. Heel (slowly at first) in a straight line, and then take small steps to the right, keeping your head, shoulders, body *and* feet pointed forward. (For those of you who ride hors-

Fading to the right—note that my feet and shoulders are facing forward and my feet are crossed. I am patting my hip to further encourage Beau to move with me. Photo: A. Kelly.

es, think *side pass*.) Pat your left leg as you move to the right and click and treat as your dog moves in to you. You can even cross your left leg in front of your right leg (all the while keeping all of your body parts straight) so that your pace remains the same and your steps don't become too large at this point.

Big step to the right (you can see Beau leaning in to me)...

...and I keep going without putting my left foot down. Photos: A. Kelly.

Gradually make your steps wider and wider, making sure you don't graduate to bigger steps until your dog is staying with you on the smaller ones. Set your dog up to succeed and don't move on to the next step until he has mastered the current one.

"Big Step to the Right" Game

Your next step is basically the final one. You have practiced doing steadily larger steps to the right and now your dog is ready to make the "big step." Your step should be as big as you can with it still being comfortable—you don't need to do a cheerleader split. Step off with your right foot, bring your left foot parallel to your right one (don't put it down on the ground) and continue heeling.

If you wish, you can name this. I use the words "get close," but you can say anything you want to. As always, be sure to name it only when it is perfect.

STRAIGHT FIGURE 8

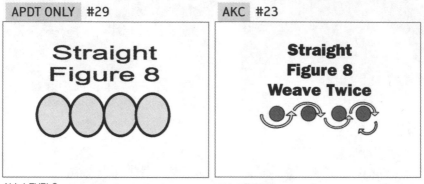

APDT ONLY #29

Straight Figure 8

ALL LEVELS

AKC #23

Straight Figure 8 Weave Twice

ALL LEVELS

Don't be fooled into thinking this is a figure 8 like in competition obedience—it isn't. You will recognize all four of these exercises by the four cones set up in a row, rather than the three cones that accompany the spiral signs. This is really a glorified "four chairs in a row" game without the "pressure" of the chairs. Beginning with the first cone to your left, you weave through the cones; as you round the last cone, you go back the way you came, again weaving around the cones. For the serpentine, you do not weave back through—you go through just once (hence, the "weave once" on the sign). You *always* start the exercise with the first cone on your left (just like weave poles in agility).

SERPENTINE WEAVE ONCE

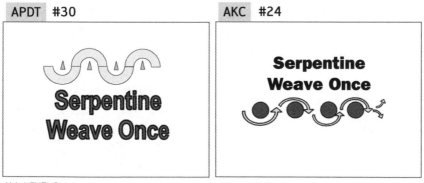

APDT #30

Serpentine Weave Once

ALL LEVELS

AKC #24

Serpentine Weave Once

ALL LEVELS

As with all of the other stations, try not to rush through this—take your time. If you remember your footwork and head and shoulder cues, your dog won't lag, forge, go too wide or bump your leg. Be sure that you don't take big steps off to the right or left—stay on track, squeezing your knees if needed so that you don't go too wide.

Correct entrance on the cones.
Photo: V. Wind.

OFFSET FIGURE 8

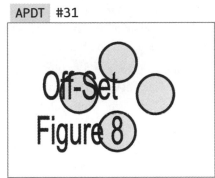

APDT #31

LEVELS 2 & 3

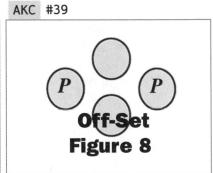

AKC #39

ADVANCED & EXCELLENT LEVELS

The offset figure 8 is probably the hardest one to train. You will essentially be heeling in a figure 8 around two posts. That's the easy part. However, in AKC, two food bowls *with* food (or toys) in them will be off to the side; in APDT, you will be heeling around four food bowls. To make matters slightly more difficult, your dog will be off leash during this exercise.

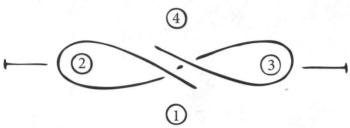

Diagram for the offset figure 8.

Training this exercise will help you in real life situations, not just the competition ring. There are three components to teaching this behavior:

* Attention during heeling while yummy smells waft up from food bowls nicely placed within reach
* A solid recall away from distractions
* A solid "mine" cue (my positive version of "leave it")

These three components break down into fourteen training steps. You may think the exercise would take forever to train—it doesn't. It should take you only two to three weeks, depending on how much you practice, and the time will be well spent, considering the value of the training. The behavior has another plus— the development of doggie self-control, helpful in many areas of your dog's life.

Your basic approach here is that you will make it great fun for your dog to come away from "stuff." For the first two steps *only,* you will be dropping the food on the floor to take your dog's focus off your hand. From step 3 on, you will be handing him the treat.

1. Put a treat in your fist and present it to your dog (letting him mug your hand). The instant he moves his head or body away, click and treat, *dropping the treat on the ground*. Repeat that step until, upon seeing your hand, he is actively moving or looking away and has completely stopped mugging your hand.

2. Present your closed fist and when your dog backs away, open your hand. If he doesn't make a move for it, click and treat, *dropping the treat on the ground*. If he does move toward your hand, don't move it away, just close

your fingers. Once he backs away again, open your hand. Continue to open and close for as long as it takes to get him to move away from your *open* hand; then drop the treat on the floor.

From step 3 onward, you will not drop the food on the ground anymore; instead, you will place all of the treats directly into his mouth. This training is valuable in real life because if you happen to drop something poisonous, your dog won't divebomb it and you won't end up at the emergency vet's.

3. Place the treat on the floor and cover it with your hand. When your dog stops mugging your hand, click and pick up the treat and hand it to him. Repeat until he is actively *not* going for your hand.

4. Do the same as step 3 except now hold your hand slightly away from the treat. The goal of this step is to have your dog back away from the "naked cookie." Click and pick up the treat and hand it to him. Repeat this step until you can get your hand farther and farther away from the treat without your dog charging it.

5. Continuing with step 4, you now want your dog to look at your face (no prompting except for a whisper the first time or two) and away from the naked cookie. Click when he looks at you, and pick up the treat and hand it to him.

6. Have a treat in each hand. Hold one arm out to the side and drop the treat on the floor at the exact same moment you hand him the treat from your other hand. Then say "stay" and pick up the one you dropped and hand it to him (you don't need to click for this one unless you have a second trainer helping you). Don't block him if he charges for the one you dropped (although you can block him with the other treat) and don't say anything. Just try again. Repeat this step until he is very much holding position.

7. Now you want a longer stay before you give the dog the treat from your hand. Count to one and then give him the treat, then count to two, and so on.

You can start naming this behavior now. *As* he is wrenching his gaze from the treat to your face, say "mine!" Each time you drop a treat, say "mine" and then reinforce your dog for looking up at you.

8. Now you drop the treat and call your dog away from it as you back away. You can cheat the first few times and show him the huge wad of food you have, luring him to you as you say in a happy voice, "Mine! Come!" Again,

never block the dog—if he races to the one you dropped, just go back and repeat step 7 some more.

You will need a helper for the next few steps. Do these steps off leash—it is your relationship that should be the "force" behind controlling your dog, not the leash.

9. Throw a treat on the ground and tell your dog to "get it." Run away. Have a second person (holding some low value food and/or toy) stand in the middle of the room, directly in the path of your dog. Call your dog to you. Your friend now tries to distract your dog (be sure that your dog doesn't get the helper's treat or toy). Do *not* repeat your come cue yet—just wait. In the split second that your dog looks toward you (and he will), call him in a very happy voice. When he gets to you, give him a huge jackpot. This may take one or two or even sixty seconds—still give him a big jackpot, no matter how long it takes him the first time or two. Repeat this until your dog is actively avoiding your friend.

> Why shouldn't you block your dog? Blocking doesn't teach him any self-control. Dogs are very smart—they know when we can block and when we can't, and they will take advantage of every opportunity offered. Don't forget, they are scavengers by nature.

10. Make the reinforcers that your friend has more valuable (but be sure that you have even better stuff) and continue in the same vein.

11. Repeat the above exercise with the food or toys being placed on the ground. (Yes, your friend can block your dog for the beginning steps—dog training isn't an exact science—there are times when I break my own rules!)

12. Have your friend start to use food bowls—empty ones to start, then with a few pieces of food, always making sure you have the better stuff. Don't worry if your dog starts to backslide a little—just be more fun, run around and do silly things to attract your dog to you. Then heavily reinforce him when he does come.

Now that your dog is easily ignoring the food bowl, we can get back to this exercise as it relates to Rally. At an actual trial, the food bowls are covered with a screen or rows of tape, but I want you to train this without those aids.

13. Place four empty bowls in a row and heel your dog past them. Start at a far distance and heavily reinforce him each time you successfully pass a bowl. If you need to, I will allow you to cheat slightly in the beginning and run past the bowls.

When you are calling your dog, use a happy voice. Don't be your mother ("Richard! You are really in for it now! I said, come here, *now!!!*" Stamp, stamp!), be Ed McMahon ("Zelda! You just won a million dollars in Publisher's Clearing House!!!!! Wahoo! Come and get your check!").

Gradually get closer and closer, making sure your reinforcers are really good ones. You can say "mine" as you are going past each bowl, *before* he may charge over to it. At this stage of the game, saying the cue "mine" *after* his face is stuck in the bowl would be setting him up to fail. Be sure that you click and reinforce him for looking away from the bowl—you may have to be really quick in your timing and reinforce him for even a split second of attention. The next step is to have food in one of the bowls and repeat step 13, then food in two of the bowls, and so on, until all of the bowls have food in them. Start with boring dry kibble in the bowls while you have the "big guns"—steak, liver, cheese, whatever your dog loves most in the world.

14. Once your dog is comfortably and reliably passing the filled food bowls, you can arrange them in the proper pattern (see diagram) and heel around them.

For these beginning stages, please use plenty of reinforcers; however, be aware that you will need to wean off food as a reinforcer for most of these exercises. In APDT Rally you can enter into the food class, but there are only certain stations where you will be allowed to use food (and this isn't one of them). In AKC Rally, no food is allowed. Since both venues allow praise and verbal encouragement, get your dog used to these reinforcers now.

Heeling around the food bowls. Photo: A. Kelly.

THIS WAY AND THAT

Some of the behaviors in this next group are beginning-level and some are higher-level exercises. They all require a bit of flexibility on the part of your dog. Some dogs are naturally supple while others are not; this quality can, however, be trained to a certain degree.

270 DEGREE RIGHT

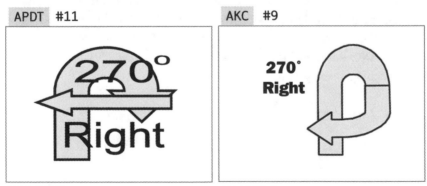

APDT #11

270°
Right

ALL LEVELS

AKC #9

270°
Right

ALL LEVELS

270 DEGREE LEFT

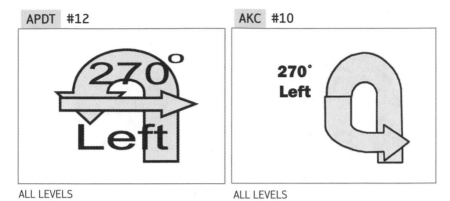

APDT #12

ALL LEVELS

AKC #10

ALL LEVELS

Because you have been working on turns, these next signs should be quite easy for you. The trickiest part is for you to remember to circle in the correct direction. Just follow the arrow! For the 270 degree turn to the right, the key is to keep your left shoulder pushed forward, your right shoulder pushed back and your head looking where you are going. For the 270 degree turn to the left, it is just the opposite: Your left shoulder is back, your right shoulder forward. If your dog is bumping you, push your left shoulder farther back and that should alleviate the problem.

If you have a small dog, you will be able to make a smaller loop. If you have a very large dog, give him a break and help him to be successful by making the circle a little larger. No matter the size of the dog, however, when beginning training for this pattern, start with a larger loop and gradually make it smaller.

360 DEGREE RIGHT

APDT #13

ALL LEVELS

AKC #11

ALL LEVELS

360 DEGREE LEFT

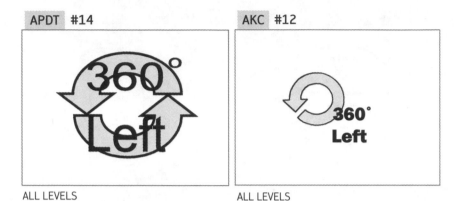

APDT #14

ALL LEVELS

AKC #12

ALL LEVELS

These signs are really quite simple—as long as you have done your home-work with your right and left turns using proper body cues. If you have a large dog, make the 360 degree left circle a little bigger to give him a chance to move his hind end out of the way. You can always practice the 360 degree to the left around a chair and click your dog for moving his hind end in. If you can't see his hind end, have someone watch and click for you.

HALT/90 DEGREE PIVOT RIGHT/HALT

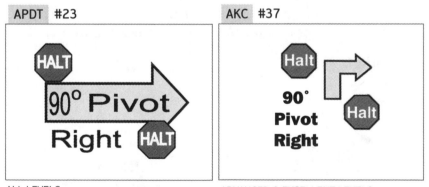

APDT #23

ALL LEVELS

AKC #37

ADVANCED & EXCELLENT LEVELS

This station is easier that it looks. You are heeling and you come to a halt. Your dog stops and sits alongside you. You then pivot *in position* to the right, and at the same time your dog comes with you and sits again. Make sure you turn in place without taking a step forward (that's a different sign). Be sure you do *not* cue your dog to heel, because that means you are going to be taking many steps forward and your dog will forge when you stop. Just use your "come up/sit" cue and he will stop when you do. You don't have to do any fancy footwork—I just do a "T" with my left foot and then place my right foot next to my left foot as I give my verbal cue.

HALT/90 DEGREE PIVOT LEFT/HALT

APDT #24

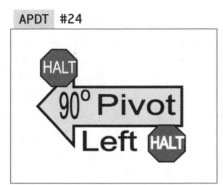

ALL LEVELS (FOOD ALLOWED)

AKC #38

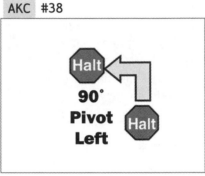

ADVANCED & EXCELLENT LEVELS

This station is much harder than the right pivot because your dog has to move his hind end back as you pivot to the left. You heel up to the sign and halt. Your dog will stop and sit. You will then pivot in place to the left and at the same time cue your dog to pivot with you. To pivot, make a "T" with your right foot in front of your left, and then place your left foot next to your right one. If your dog is supple and/or smallish, it won't be too difficult for him to move with you. If your dog is larger and/or stiffer, it won't be impossible to train, just slightly harder—you may have to lure.

You can start training this in a similar manner to that used to train the moving side step right. Play the "lean to the right" game, and once your dog is proficient at that, jump slightly to the right and pat the side of your leg to encourage your dog to scoot over with you and stay in heel position. Be sure to click and treat him for even a substandard attempt at first.

Click a substandard behavior? I have been telling you *not* to do this; however, there are times you need to reward an effort even if it isn't perfect at first. It will keep your dog motivated and excited, and you won't crush his spirit. After all, while Rally is a wonderful sport, no sport is worth de-motivating your dog. The key is to know when to raise your criteria and only click when your dog gets it correct.

Once your dog is scooting with you, start to jump *slightly* into a pivot left, continuing to pat your leg while you push your left shoulder back to encourage him to come with you. Click and treat, making sure you feed him with his head pointed to the left. That will also help get his hind end in. Continue to do this and gradually make your jump/pivot more in line with the 90 degree pivot you will need.

If your dog is having a problem with this, you can do it around a chair and click him for moving his hind end in toward you. You can use also use larger lure (luring his head to the left) at first if you need to. Once the behavior is perfect, you can name this behavior. I use the words "get close!"

HALT/180 DEGREE PIVOT RIGHT/HALT

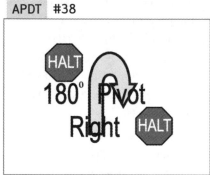

APDT #38

LEVELS 2 & 3 (FOOD ALLOWED)

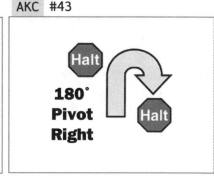

AKC #43

ADVANCED & EXCELLENT LEVELS

This is an easy exercise. Basically it is an about turn (so now you are headed back to where you just came from) without the forward heeling motion after the turn. You come to a halt and your dog sits. Place your left foot in front of your right foot in a "T" position, as you push your left shoulder forward and your

CHAPTER 5 In and Out, Back and Forth

right shoulder back (make sure your head follows your right shoulder). Put your right foot heel to heel in an "L" position, and then put your left foot next to your right one. Your dog moves with you and then sits again before moving forward on your cue. Be sure to follow through with your head and shoulder cues and just as in any of the stationary exercises, use your "come up/sit" cue, rather than your "heel" cue. You can use a verbal or hand cue reminder to sit.

HALT/180 DEGREE PIVOT LEFT/HALT

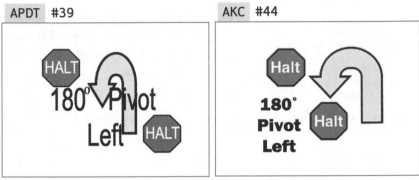

APDT #39	AKC #44
LEVELS 2 & 3 (FOOD ALLOWED)	ADVANCED & EXCELLENT LEVELS

This is quite similar to the halt/90 degree pivot left exercise, except you will be doing a full turn to head back the way you came. Just like the turn to the right, you heel up to the sign and halt. Your dog stops and sits in heel position. Pivot in place 180 degrees, stop, and have your dog sit in heel position again. Your dog should be scooting his hind end back at the same time that you are turning. You don't need to be doing any special footwork for this, but once your dog is proficient, you can name it the same ("get close!") as the 90 degree pivot to the left.

You can easily train this behavior by doing large left circles, gradually spiraling them into nice tight turns. Don't do too many in a row—otherwise you'll get dizzy. Feel free to really exaggerate your head and shoulder cues in the beginning and be sure to click and treat any inward motion of your dog's hind end—click for movement and be sure to feed him with his head out, to further encourage him to get his hind end in.

HALT/TURN RIGHT/1 STEP/HALT

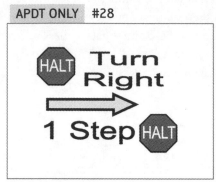

APDT ONLY   #28

ALL LEVELS (FOOD ALLOWED)

Here's an easy exercise! (After the last few difficult ones, you deserve this!) This one is almost identical to the 90 degree pivot to the right. You heel up to the sign and stop; your dog stops with you and sits in heel position. You turn to the right, take one step, and then halt again. Once you have done the other exercises and practiced your own footwork, you and your dog should ace this.

HALT/TURN RIGHT/1 STEP/CALL TO HEEL/HALT

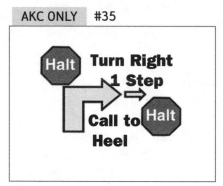

AKC ONLY   #35

ADVANCED & EXCELLENT LEVELS

You may think this sign is the same as the last one, but it isn't. Heel up to the sign and halt. Tell your dog to stay, and then pivot to the right while taking one step in that direction and halt again. At that point, call your dog to come up to sit in heel position. So, unlike the preceding one, in this exercise, your dog is not actually heeling with you.

Andrea has pivoted and taken the one step. Darcy is still in the stay.

BONUS EXERCISE: HALT/LEAVE DOG/CALL TO HEEL

APDT ONLY

BONUS

Halt
Leave Dog

BONUS

Call
To Heel

LEVEL 1

You are not required to do this exercise, and its time is not included in your course time. As with the other bonus exercises, you must let the judge know before you begin your run whether or not you will be performing the bonus exercise; you are then committed to that choice.

This exercise is almost the same as the previous one. The main difference is that you take the leash off or let it drop after you tell your dog to stay. This exercise has two signs. After crossing the finish line, you heel to the bonus exercise sign "Halt/Leave Dog." At the sign, you halt and the dog sits. Once the dog is sitting, you drop the leash or take it off and proceed to the second sign, "Call to Heel."

You stop at this sign. You do not face the dog, but instead, with your back to him, call him to move to heel position. Your dog must come promptly and sit at heel position. You may cue the dog to sit at heel. Once sitting at heel, you pick up the leash and the exercise is considered complete.

To make this easier for your dog, use your left hand when you call him to heel position to make sure to he comes to heel position and not to your right.

RALLY AROUND

- Be sure to practice your footwork and body postures without your dog. Once you are proficient, then you can add your dog. If at any time your dog is bumping, lagging or forging, look to your own body cues.
- When working on ignoring dropped food in preparation for the offset figure 8, be sure that you don't yell at your dog if he happens to get the treat. Have patience and just try again.

chapter

TAKING IT TO THE NEXT LEVEL

Most of the exercises in this chapter are in both APDT level 2 and AKC Advanced. Most of them are quite easy to train, so don't let yourself be intimidated. Some are similar to what you have already learned and several are completely different—but that's what keeps you on your toes! The first three signs here are related to what you previously learned. The last signs are completely new behaviors.

SIMPLE COMBINATIONS

HALT/FROM SIT ABOUT TURN RIGHT & FORWARD

APDT #40

HALT From Sit About Turn Right & Forward

LEVELS 2 & 3

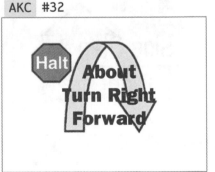

AKC #32

Halt About Turn Right Forward

ADVANCED & EXCELLENT LEVELS

This exercise is really just an about turn from a sit and then you keep heeling to the next sign. You stop moving, and your dog sits. You do your about turn footwork without your dog sitting again, and off you go! How simple is *that*?

HALT/FROM SIT ABOUT U TURN & FORWARD

APDT #41

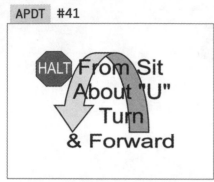

LEVELS 2 & 3

AKC #33

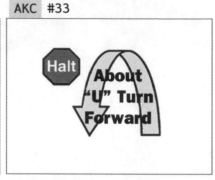

ADVANCED & EXCELLENT LEVELS

This is the opposite of the previous sign. You come to a halt and your dog sits. Then you do a left U turn and keep heeling. The size of the U really depends on the size and flexibility of your dog. The tighter the better, but don't become neurotic if you have a huge Newfoundland and think he has to turn as tightly as the twelve-inch Shetland Sheepdog.

HALT/SIDE STEP RIGHT/HALT

APDT #47

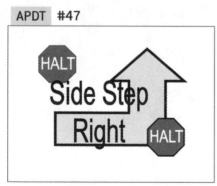

LEVELS 2 & 3

AKC #40

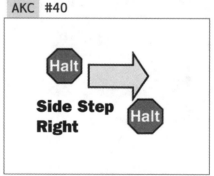

ADVANCED & EXCELLENT LEVELS

This is the same as the side step right sign in the beginning levels, except there is a halt on each end. Halt, take a big step to the right and stop again. Your dog must move with you as you move to the right and sit again when you stop.

JUMPING

SEND OVER JUMP/HANDLER RUNS BY

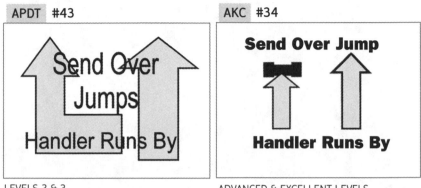

APDT #43	AKC #34
LEVELS 2 & 3	ADVANCED & EXCELLENT LEVELS

I personally love this exercise. The first time we had this at a trial, Shadow was sorely disappointed that there weren't any more jumps. He erroneously thought that all of a sudden the Rally course had turned into agility!

The exercise looks like this: You approach the sign and start to run along the line that has been conveniently marked on the floor or grass for you. Your dog runs parallel to you as you run along this line, and you signal him to go over the jump. The two of you catch up to each other on the other side of it. Two factors give this exercise an interesting slant: the line is six feet away from the jump, and if your dog is really fast, you have to be even faster to meet up with him after the jump. After that, you heel calmly to the next sign.

You will train this in small steps. If your dog doesn't know how to jump, start with the steps immediately below. If your dog already jumps easily, skip this part and go on to the next. If you already run your dog in agility, this exercise will take you about one minute to train.

BEGINNING JUMPING

1. Put the jump at a height of eight inches (no matter the size of your dog, although if your dog is really small, make the jump four inches).
2. Have your dog off leash and on your left side.

Andrea is running and signaling Flute to jump. Note the line on the ground (the handler's path) and that Andrea's arm signal is given when the dog is still some distance away from the jump.

Andrea and Flute meeting up after the jump.

3. *Walk* up to the jump (with you on the right side of the jump) and toss a treat over the jump with your left hand, encouraging your dog to go over it. When he does, click and he'll get the treat.

When tossing the treat, make sure it goes fairly far (at least eight feet) past the jump so that your dog can learn to jump properly and land safely. Many dogs have a hard time finding treats in grass, so be sure to use light colored treats. You can also use heavier type of treats, such as tortellini or big chunks of cheese, for ease of throwing.

4. Repeat this numerous times until your dog does not hesitate to jump.

5. Now it's time to get rid of the food. Walk up to the jump and use the same hand movement with your left hand that you used when tossing the food. Your dog should go over the jump. Once he has cleared the jump, click and toss a treat in his path using your *right* hand.

6. You can start naming this behavior now. The most common cues are "hup," "over," or simply "jump." Say the word *as* your dog is going over the jump.

Andrea tossing the treat at a far enough distance that Darcy can land safely and not cut the jump short.

7. Your dog is now going over the jump with ease. I want you to continue walking with him; if you don't, he may have a tendency to stop his jump short and hurt himself or drop the bar. Since the exercise ends with you meeting up with your dog on the far side of the jump, you may as well teach him this from the beginning.

INTERMEDIATE JUMPING

1. Jog slowly toward the jump, repeating the same final steps from above (use your left hand to signal the dog, say your verbal cue, fling the treat with your right hand and meet up with your dog after he jumps).

2. Jog faster, repeating the above step.

3. Run, repeating the above step.

ADVANCED JUMPING

Mark off different distances from the side of the jump—one, two, three feet, and so on, until you have reached six feet. Make your lines long so *you* learn to run in a straight line.

Note the lines marked on the ground for the approximations.

AKC RALLY JUMP SPECIFICS

In AKC, the jump may be any jump used as standard equipment in AKC obedience classes (broad jump, high jump, or bar jump), except that four-foot wide jumps may be used in place of five-foot wide jumps. Various colors and decorations are allowed; however, there must be nothing hanging from the jump.

The **broad jump** consists of three telescoping hurdles, each approximately eight inches wide. The largest hurdle measures about four feet ten inches long (if from a five-foot set) and about five inches at the highest point. In the ring, broad jump hurdles are arranged in order of size from smallest to largest. They are evenly spaced, covering a distance equal to twice the height of the high jump set for each dog. Three hurdles will be used for a jump of thirty-two inches and two hurdles for a jump of sixteen or twenty-four inches. When decreasing the number of hurdles in the jump, the highest hurdle is removed first.

The **high jump** consists of two uprights and solid boards of varying widths that combine to make each dog's required jump height.

The **bar jump** also has two uprights. These are constructed to support only a striped bar which is set at the dog's required jump height.

1. Start on the one-foot line approximately ten feet back from the jump.

2. Run toward the jump, and when you are still about eight to ten feet away, say your dog's name and your jump word.

3. You want to give him the jump cue way before he gets to the jump—if you give your signal too late, he may crash into the jump or go around it.

4. Once your dog is successfully going over the jump as you stay on your line one foot away, go to two feet away. Be sure that you stay on your line and that you give your dog the hand and verbal signals ahead of time. You'll know if your timing is off if your dog misses the jump.

5. Repeat the exercise, graduating one foot at a time until you are six feet away and your dog is jumping happily and accurately.

If at any time your dog misses the jump, just backtrack a foot or so until he remembers what do to.

The second half of this exercise is racing past the jump to meet up with your dog and then easing into a comfortable normal heeling pace. This is easy to accomplish. Click your dog for going over the jump and then give him a treat at your side. Very quickly he will learn to come to you after clearing the jump. If your dog is faster than you and he goes past you slightly, it is no big deal; just call him to heel, and he will adjust his pace to yours.

JUMP HEIGHTS

	DOG'S HEIGHT AT WITHERS	JUMP HEIGHT
APDT RALLY	under 12 inches	4 inches
	from 12 to under 16 inches	8 inches
	from 16 to under 20 inches	12 inches
	20 inches or more	16 inches
AKC RALLY	under 15 inches	8 inches
	15 to under 20 inches	12 inches
	20 inches or more	16 inches

Note: The maximum jump height in both venues is 16 inches.

Up to now, you have kept the jump height at eight inches so as not to put extra pressure on your dog's body while the two of you are learning something new. Now that you and your dog are doing the entire exercise correctly, you may ease into the correct height for your dog. When I say "ease" I do mean *ease*. If your dog will be jumping the maximum height of sixteen inches, first go to twelve inches and make sure he is comfortable there before going to the full height.

In APDT Level 3, the courses must include two jumps in any combination from levels 2 and 3. In AKC Rally, the Advanced class must include one jump. The Excellent class must include two jumps; these may not be used consecutively on the course. In AKC, the jump can be a broad jump instead of a bar jump. The broad jump will cover a distance equal to twice the height of the high jump setting for each dog. Thus, for instance, if your dog measures twenty inches, the broad jump will be thirty-two inches. Two hurdles are used for distances of sixteen to twenty-four inches and three hurdles are used for disances of thirty-two inches.

In agility, one of the keys to not taking a bar down or missing an obstacle is to get your cue word/signal out almost before the dog is even done with the previous jump. If you wait until he is nearly at the jump, he will not have enough time to properly and safely take off. The same timing holds for Rally jumps.

ADDING SPEED

HALT/LEAVE/CALL FRONT WHILE RUNNING

#44

LEVELS 2 & 3 (FOOD ALLOWED IF END WITH RIGHT OR LEFT FINISH. IF A FORWARD, THEN FOOD IS NOT ALLOWED)

You heel up to the sign, stop, and your dog sits. Tell your dog to stay, and then you run two to three steps. As you are *still* running, you will call your dog to come and as he catches up with you, you will back up a step or two and call him to front position. If you have a slow dog, don't run too fast. (If you have a fast dog, don't worry about it.)

When you start to train this, your dog may very well run and chase you even though you asked him to stay. This is no big deal. Just take one running step and then run back and click and treat him for staying. Do this a few times until he is consistently not moving. Then run two steps, and click and go back and reinforce. Once you can run about four or five steps with your dog sitting like a

I am running while Beau stays in place. Photo: A. Kelly.

rock, call him to you. You may want to put your left hand out as a target so the dog knows what side to come to. You can do this at a trial as well.

Once you have called your dog and he comes running to your left side, you back up a few steps, call the dog to front and have him sit. The next sign on the course will tell you what to do after this—a left or right finish or forward.

HALT/FAST FORWARD FROM SIT

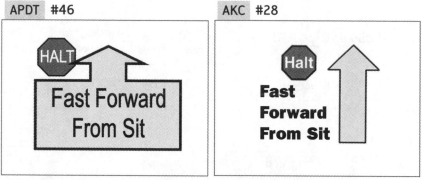

LEVELS 2 & 3   NOVICE LEVEL ON LEASH

Heel up to the sign and halt. Your dog sits. Then you run (don't walk) a few steps and, this time, your dog stays with you.

The easiest way to train this is to verbally rev up your dog ("Are you ready?!") with a happy voice, and then run one step and click and treat him if he stays with you. You can also throw the treat ahead of you as a further reward for the fast forward movement. Do not throw the treat ahead if he is lagging—if you do, as you already now know, you are actually reinforcing him for lagging.

You can also lean forward slightly before taking off, as an additional signal to your dog that you are going to be burning rubber.

Once you have that first running step, add in a second step, then a third and so on, always clicking and reinforcing your dog for staying with you in heel position.

If you have a Mr. Speedy dog, click and treat him *before* he forges and be sure to feed in heel position. You can also adjust your stride a little and take smaller steps—not slower, just smaller steps.

HALT/STAND WITH DISTRACTION

RETURN AND FORWARD FROM STAND

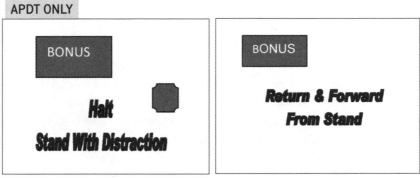

APDT ONLY

BONUS

Halt

Stand With Distraction

BONUS

Return & Forward
From Stand

LEVEL 3 BONUS

If you have trained Novice in competition obedience, you already know this exercise. The only differences are that here, there is no actual exam—the judge just walks around your dog and you do *not* wait to hear "return to your dog," and once you return to heel position, you do *not* wait for the judge to say "exercise finished." (Otherwise you'll be waiting all day for something you'll never hear, and the spectators will be sending you urgent mental messages to "Go back to your dog!") If it seems like it is taking an inordinate amount of time for the judge to say these things or you happen to glance at the people outside the ring and see their eyes bugging out of their heads, that will be your cue to remember you are doing Rally, not competition obedience.

You halt and your dog sits. Stand your dog (see instructions in Chapter 3), tell him to stay, and then walk out six feet, turn, and face

You may have noticed that I am asking for much more from the dog than will be required at a trial. Ask anyone who competes—you always want to train to a higher level than you'll need. That way, when at a trial, the actual exercises are much easier for your dog to perform and he will be more successful. For example, many people will train a two-minute sit stay for Novice competition obedience, when a one-minute is all that is needed.

your dog. The judge will then walk around your dog. As soon the judge is done, go back around your dog so that you end up in heel position.

I train this the same way whether working with a confident or a nervous dog. If you have the former, this will go quickly. If you have the latter, you will need to build up your dog's confidence so he knows that the judge is not out to get him or do bad things to him. An overly friendly dog (which is most likely a dog that also lacks confidence) can also benefit from these steps.

If you think your dog is too nervous to handle this right now, just simply tell the judge that you will not be doing the bonus exercise. You risk a dog bite report and having your dog banned forever from the sport—not something you want to risk. Make sure you have a solid foundation of desensitization before attempting this exercise. (See Appendix 3 for more information on desensitization.)

You need a helper to train this behavior:

1. Signal your dog to stand.

2. Move directly in front of him.

3. Have your helper walk around your dog, about one to ten feet away (or more), depending on the comfort level of your dog.

4. If your dog glances at your helper and then looks back to you, click and treat.

5. Repeat the above step, always clicking and treating for eye contact.

6. After a few minutes, your dog will most likely not even bother to look at your helper.

Andrea is walking around Beau, while he stares at me.

Photo: P. Kelly.

Why click and treat for eye contact throughout this exercise? If your dog is staring at you, he will be less likely to move toward, jump on, or move away from the judge.

In your next training session:

1. Repeat the above steps to refresh your dog's memory—one or two repetitions is enough.

2. Now have your helper come a little closer to the dog.

3. Continue to click and treat for your dog's eye contact with you.

As long as your dog continues to be comfortable, you can move on to the next steps. Be sure to break them down into a few sessions—don't try to get them all in one day. Too much standing still, especially if your dog is a little nervous or very energetic, is very hard. Be sure to break up this stationary exercise with some play.

4. Have your helper walk directly at your dog from the front and both sides. Click and treat for eye contact with you.

5. Repeat a few times until your dog is completely ignoring your helper and boring holes in your head.

6. Your helper can now start to make it a little harder in a step-by-step way—wearing a big hat; holding a clipboard, coming a little closer;—all the while you continue to click and treat for calm eye contact with you.

 Herding breeds tend to be more "pressure sensitive" and may need more room at the start of this training. At first, my Border Collie Beau needed a good twenty-to twenty-five-foot distance from our helper for him to remain in position. Don't think you have a stupid or stubborn dog—these breeds were developed to be this way, to respond to pressure of the flock. That's what makes them so good at their job.

RALLY AROUND

* The training of the exercises in this chapter may seem hard—they aren't. Move step by step, and you'll be surprised at how quickly your dog learns them.

* If your dog is nervous about the stand for exam exercise, take it very slowly. You do not want him to attach a bad association to people approaching and touching him.

* Always train for more than you need!

← 7 →

COMPLEX MANEUVERS

The exercises in this chapter are the hardest ones to train, although I find them the most fun both to teach and to do. (Call me crazy, but that is what makes training so challenging (in a good way)—working out the hard stuff.) I use many of these behaviors in day-to-day living. For instance, I often signal my dogs to do the moving stand when I want to let one dog out but not the others. I use "directionals" to get my dogs move or look away from something potentially scary, thus avoiding problems.

STAND STILL, SOLDIER

MOVING STAND/WALK AROUND

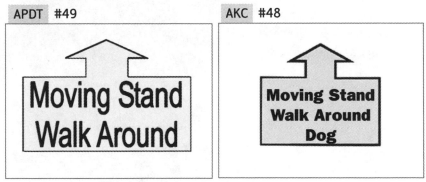

APDT #49	AKC #48
LEVEL 3	EXCELLENT LEVEL

Heel up to the sign, and signal your dog to stand (no sitting first). Then, with no hesitation, walk around your dog, go back to heel position and continue heeling to the next exercise.

For training purposes, you will break this exercise into two components—the stand/stay and the walking around. If you have done your homework with your stand, this may be quite simple for your dog. Heel off slowly, and with your right hand, signal (hand and/or verbal) your dog to stand and stay. If he hesitates for even a second, click and treat (you go back to him to treat). If he doesn't hesitate, give your hand signal again and see if that works, making sure you click and treat any hesitation. Most of the time, your dog will stop his forward movement at the second signal.

Once you have the stand/stay part, the walk around should be pretty easy. If you have worked on the stand for exam already, you won't have any problem with this at all. If you haven't worked the "return to heel position," go back to the section that teaches the "walk around" for the sit and down in Chapter 4 and now practice it with the stand.

I am signaling Shadow to do the stand/stay. Photo: V. Wind.

Andrea walking around Darcy while she is standing.

MOVING STAND/LEAVE DOG/
TURN AND CALL TO HEEL

APDT ONLY #50   #51

LEVEL 3

There are two signs for this exercise. As in the previous exercise, you signal your dog to stand/stay. You then leave your dog and walk out approximately six to ten feet. Turn and face the dog and call him to heel position without coming to front first. The dog doesn't have to sit in heel position, but he may. You both then heel to the next sign.

To train this, don't walk out the six to ten feet in the beginning—just go out about one foot and, with a big arm movement to start, signal your dog to get into heel position. You are allowed to signal the right or left finish for this. I use the right finish hand and verbal signal with my dogs. For some reason this seems to be easier for them to understand than doing a left finish. Gradually increase your distance by one foot at a time until you are at the required distance.

I am facing Shadow and signaling him to come to heel (he is bypassing the front.) Photo: V. Wind.

MOVING STAND/LEAVE DOG
TURN AND DOWN/SIT/CALL/FINISH

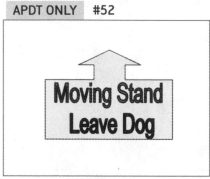

APDT ONLY #52

Moving Stand
Leave Dog

#53

Turn and
Down,
Sit,
Call,
Finish

LEVEL 3 (FOOD ALLOWED)

This exercise also has two signs. It begins the same way as number 50, with the moving stand. You leave your dog in a stand/stay, walk out six to ten feet, and turn and face your dog. You then cue your dog to lie down, then sit, and then come front. Once the dog is sitting front, you cue him to do the right or left finish at your discretion.

For those of you who have trained for utility, this is the same as the signal exercise except that you are allowed to use your voice as well as hand signals and the distance is not as great.

You will need some additional hand signals for this exercise, although you can simply use verbal ones if you wish. I find it easier to use hand plus verbal signals or just hand signals alone. The most common down signal is to raise your hand like a traffic cop. The sit signal can be an exaggerated lure, palm up, starting from your waist and rising upward. The come signal can just be a voice cue, since most likely your dog is already good at it, or you can also make a sweeping motion with your hand, bringing your arm out and around so that your hand ends up on your chest. To make it more unmistakable for my dogs, I use my right hand for the down, left hand for the sit and right hand again for the come. Once your dog is sitting front, do whichever finish your dog does better.

To teach your dog that a raised hand means to lie down, start with your dog directly in front of you. You may want to practice this from a stand since that is what your dog will be doing right before you cue him to lie down. No matter what signal your dog knows now, the steps are still the same:

The most common hand signal for the down.
Notice that Andrea's arm is held high so Quigley can see it.

The exaggerated sit signal.

1. Present your new cue first.
2. Wait about two seconds and present your old cue.
3. Click and treat for the down.
4. Repeat this about six to ten times.
5. Now present only the new cue and wait.
6. If your dog does the down, click and jackpot! If your dog doesn't go down after about ten seconds, utilize your old cue but make it smaller. If your old cue is verbal, whisper "down." If your old cue is a different hand signal, such as pointing to the ground, make it a smaller hand signal. Repeat this a few more times, giving your dog more time to think about the new cue, and making your helper cue smaller and smaller.

Once your dog is responding to the new cue, put him in a stand/stay and move about one foot away and repeat the down signal. Gradually go farther away until you are at the required six to ten feet. If at any time your dog creeps forward to do the down or tries to sit first, just review the behavior from a closer distance for a few more repetitions. Make sure you always go to him to deliver the reinforcer.

CHANGING A CUE
Whenever you want to rename or give a new signal to an already existing behavior, always present the new cue first and then the old one. This would not apply to a cue that is "poisoned," such as dog that runs away when you say "come." In that case, you would just rename it without saying the old cue.

Your sit cue will be easy since you already used a lure/hand signal to teach the sit. This will really be about adding two new aspects to the sit: having your dog sit from a down and having him sit at a distance.

Practice the sit from a down first with your dog in front of you. As in the previous step, once your dog has mastered this, increase your distance in small increments until you are at the required distance.

The come part is pretty easy since you don't have to add in a new signal—you can just call your dog to come. Then it will be your choice as to which way to finish your dog—right or left.

PUT IT IN REVERSE

MOVING BACKUP/HEEL BACK 3 STEPS THEN FORWARD

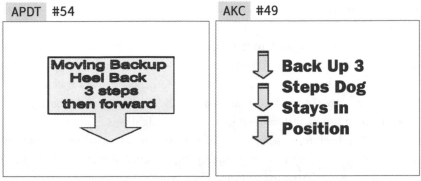

APDT #54

LEVEL 3

AKC #49

EXCELLENT LEVEL

While heeling, you will cue your dog to back up from a standing position. Essentially you will be backing up for three steps with your dog remaining in heel position. Once you have completed the three steps, you will just continue to heel backward for the entire balance of the course. (Ha! Gotcha! Only kidding—just making sure you were paying attention.). After the three steps, you will then heel forward to the next sign. Sitting is not allowed at all during this exercise.

You can train this with or without props, depending on your own skills and those of your dog.

CALL FRONT/BACKUP 3 STEPS

APDT ONLY

LEVEL 3 BONUS

For this bonus exercise, you heel up to the sign, then back up while calling the dog to front position. After he sits, you then ask him to back up while you walk toward him for three steps. The judge will be counting your steps, not your dog's. It's a pretty easy sign, but the catch is that he must stay straight while backing up. You also need to be careful that he doesn't back up into the sign and knock it over.

Start with your dog standing in front and have a treat in each hand. Keep your hands relatively flat (not in a fist), bring both hands down toward his chest/shoulder area and make a "shooing" motion with your hands. If he leans back or moves even one step, "yes" and treat. (Too hard to use a clicker for this one). Should he sit, just ask him to stand again and lower your hands a little bit more so he continues to stand. Don't try to get all three steps all at once. Work on straight first, then ask for additional steps. Many people use a wall to get the dog to back up straight, but I feel that muddies up the waters and it is hard to fade the wall. Using two hands will help him to stay straight.

Once he is backing up straight, you'll need to fade your hand signal to something smaller. Gradually raise your hands higher until you reach about waist level, still doing your shooing motion. Then you can get the food out of your hands. If you want to give this a verbal cue, name it when it is perfect. Common words to use are "back" or "beep, beep, beep" (like a truck backing up).

Using Props

Get two baby gates and line them up in two parallel lines about two feet apart (use more or less space depending upon the size of your dog). Position yourself so the gates are on your left. Encourage your dog to go straight through them, and click and treat at the end. Repeat about three to four times so that the dog isn't nervous about the gates.

You now walk slowly up to the gates, put your hand with a treat down to your dog's nose and lure him in one step. Then lure him backward, as you also take one step back. Click and treat for any backward movement. You will have to position your lure hand so that he doesn't sit or lie down—it may take a few repetitions to get it right. For most dogs, it works best if you position your hand just a hair lower than where your stand signal is.

Repeat the one step forward and one step backward a few more times, then go for two steps, then three, and so on. Once your dog is doing it instantly, you can name it. The most common cue word is "back," although my personal favorite is "beep, beep, beep" (like a truck backing up). You now must fade the props. Take out the gate closest to you and repeat the exercise a few times; then get rid of the second gate. Your dog may tend to crab his hind end out—just reposition your hand slightly to the outside to keep his hind end straight.

Two baby gates. Notice that Andrea is luring Quigley in a short distance...

...and then luring him backward.

Without Props

You can follow the same procedure as above, only without the gates. Position your hand so that your dog backs up. Don't try to go for all three steps at once, but break the training down into tiny pieces—one step or even a half step of backward movement at a time. There are two criteria here: backing up and backing up straight.

For either option (props or no props), you must fade your hand signal to a more manageable cue. An easy hand cue is to put your left hand at your side with your palm facing down so the dog has something to target.

Luring the backing up with no props. Notice that Andrea's hand position ensures that Quigley will back straight.

A FEW MORE SIMPLE PATTERNS

HALT/LEAVE DOG/RECALL

#34

LEVELS 2 & 3 (FOOD ALLOWED)

TURN & CALL FRONT

#35

LEVELS 2 & 3 (FOOD ALLOWED)

FINISH RIGHT/LEFT

#36

#37

LEVELS 2 & 3 (FOOD ALLOWED)

This is a simple recall exercise. Three signs are needed for this exercise: numbers 34 and 35, plus either 36 or 37. The first sign tells you to halt and have the dog sit in heel position. Ask your dog to stay and walk to the "turn and call front" sign. Be sure to leave your dog enough room so that when you do ask him to finish, he won't knock over the sign behind you. Face your dog and call him to come. He must sit when he comes in and be close enough so that if you wanted to, you could touch his collar or head. Then do the right or left finish as dictated by the next sign.

BONUS EXERCISE: HALT/LEAVE DOG/ RECALL TURN AND CALL FRONT/ FINISH R/L

LEVEL 1 BONUS

This bonus is just a simple recall exercise. You stop at the first sign, ask your dog to sit and then stay. Walk to the next sign, face your dog and then call him to front. You have the option of doing a right or left finish. As with all exercises that have a finish, be sure to give your dog room to do it so he doesn't knock the sign over.

BONUS EXERCISE: HALT/LEAVE DOG TURN CALL FRONT

LEVEL 2 BONUS

CH 7 Complex Maneuvers

This bonus is the same as a regular recall except the judge walks past your dog as he is coming to you. The arrow on the sign will remind you that it is a recall with distractions. You'll need to practice this in case your dog is the type that gets easily distracted.

LIAR'S GAME (COME WITH DISTRACTIONS)

Come with distractions is probably the most important behavior you will teach your dog—in or out of the ring. This game teaches the dog that you are always a "sure bet" and everyone else in the world is a liar.

1. Have someone hold your dog or do a sit stay.
2. Have a second person (this is "the liar") stand in the middle of the room and give them some food or toys. Start with something of relatively low value to the dog. We want to set him up for success!
3. You go across the room or yard.
4. Call your dog to come.
5. The liar tries to distract the dog. The liar does NOT let the dog have the goodies or give the dog eye contact.
6. Do NOT repeat your cue—just wait.
7. When dog comes to you, click and treat with a huge jackpot.
8. Repeat a bunch of times until the dog is actively ignoring the "liar."

Practice this enough and your dog will do it perfectly—in the ring and in real life!

RIGHT TURN/1-2 STEPS/ DOWN DOG/FORWARD

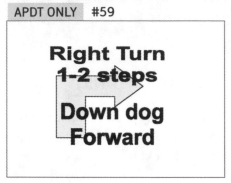

LEVEL 3

LEFT TURN/1-2 STEPS/ DOWN DOG/FORWARD

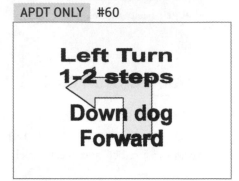

LEVEL 3

This is really just a moving down after a turn to the right or left. You will make a right or left turn, take one or two steps, do your moving down (see sign number 45 in Chapter 4 for instructions on how to train the moving down), and then heel to the next sign.

JUMPING JIMINY

HALT/LEAVE DOG/RECALL OVER JUMP

TURN/CALL OVER JUMP/FINISH OR FORWARD

LEVEL 3 (FOOD ALLOWED ONLY IF YOU USE THE FINISH (SIT) OPTION)

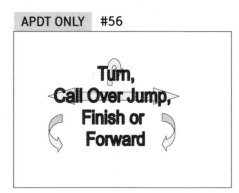

There are two signs needed for this exercise. You heel up to and halt at a spot approximately fifteen feet away from the center of the jump. Your dog sits and you ask him to stay. Walk to the other side of the jump, directly opposite your dog. Turn and face your dog and call him to you over the jump. He comes in and sits front. You have the option to do a finish (with a sit) or a forward (no sit) in either direction—right or left.

Make sure your dog is comfortable jumping before doing this exercise. (See Chapter 6 for jumping instructions.) Try this one time to see if your dog goes around the jump or over it. If he goes over the jump, you've got it. If he goes around, you need a little training. Set him up a little closer to the jump (about seven to eight feet away), tell him to stay, and go to the opposite side of the jump. Tap on the jump bar, and back away and call him to jump—and get out of his way. Be sure you move far enough away so he can land properly. Do this a few times and then just point to the bar and ask him to jump. Little by little increase the distance until both you and he are at the required fifteen feet from your respective sides of the jump.

HALT/LEAVE DOG/SEND OVER JUMP

TURN AND SEND OVER JUMP/ FINISH OR FORWARD

APDT ONLY #57

#58

LEVEL 3 (FOOD ALLOWED ONLY IF YOU CHOOSE THE FINISH (SIT) OPTION)

This is another exercise that utilizes two signs. Be careful not to confuse these signs with those of the previous exercise. Basically, you halt at the first sign at a spot approximately twenty feet away from the jump and eight feet to either the right or left side of the jump, depending on the course layout. Tell your dog

Proper position of handler and dog in relation to the jump.

to stay, and walk to the second sign, approximately twenty feet away on the other side of the jump, directly opposite your dog. (You will both be off center of the jump.) Send your dog over the jump. As the dog is in the air, turn and face him so he can do a straight front with a sit. Then you have the option to finish or forward to the right or left. For those of you who have trained directed jumping in utility, that's what this is, but without the go-out. For those of you who haven't— read on.

The description for this training this may seem endless, but the actual training itself doesn't take all that long—approximately two weeks or so depending on how much you practice.

There are a few parts to this exercise:

➤ Teaching your dog to go in the direction you are pointing.
➤ Teaching your dog to jump the jump in the direction you are pointing rather than coming in straight to you and bypassing the jump.

Direction

Let's train the "directed" portion first so your dog knows you want him to move in the direction you are pointing. Without using a jump, have a bunch of treats in your right hand and a clicker in your left. Face your dog, and with your right hand point to the right (be sure to look in the direction you are pointing,

I am pointing and Shadow is moving in that direction.
Photo: V. Wind.

not at your dog). If he looks to the right, click and toss a treat in that direction. If he stands there staring at you, make sure you aren't staring at him; look at where you are pointing.

If your peripheral vision isn't all that great, you may need someone to help you click when the dog turns his head. Your dog will likely get the concept if you move your arm and hand in a quick movement—too slow and he won't see it. If your dog looks at your hand, don't click, just try again. Make sure your pointer finger is pointing—if you use your entire hand in a fist, he won't see it. (Don't ask me why—I have no idea why this works better, I just know, after teaching hundreds of dogs, that it does.) Repeat about a dozen times, and then switch hands and point to your left. You may find that your dog does this better on one side than the other—this is normal. Use your right hand for pointing to the right and left hand for the left; don't mix them up—it will only confuse your dog. Most dogs will start to move in the direction you are pointing to get the treat faster—like the outfielder who runs to catch the ball.

Directed Jumping

Your dog is now moving in the direction you are pointing. Let's work on using your right hand for now.

1. Set up a very low jump, put your dog into a stay on one side of it (centered and approximately eight feet away) and you go to the opposite side, slightly closer to the jump than he is. Stand slightly off-center and to the left. Cue your dog to jump, using your word and your right arm motion. Repeat twice.

2. Do the same thing except take one medium step to the left.

Quigley is centered on jump, while Andrea is off to one side, giving an exaggerated cue.

Quigley is now off-center and the cue is less exaggerated.

3. Repeat this, moving one medium step to the left each time, until you are eight feet to the left of the jump.

If you have to, by all means lean into your "point" as you build your distance away from center to help your dog. Then gradually wean off the helper cue.

The next step is to start moving your dog off center as well. Step by step, place him farther to the right (his right) of the jump. Make sure you go back to using a helper cue as you both become more in line.

Once you are both in line—you to the left of the jump and your dog facing you (from his direction, he will be to the right of the jump)—and he is consistently jumping the jump, you can begin teaching this exercise from the opposite side. Start at the very beginning of the steps outlined here when changing direction. It will go very quickly, so don't try to cut corners. Because the direction of jumps varies depending on course design, you and your dog need to be proficient with both the right and left sides. Gradually raise the jump to the proper height once your dog is comfortable with this exercise.

DROP ON RECALL

HALT/LEAVE DOG/DOWN ON RECALL

TURN/RECALL/DOWN/RECALL/FINISH OR FORWARD

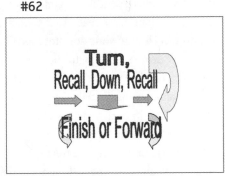

LEVEL 3 (FOOD ALLOWED ONLY IF YOU CHOOSE THE FINISH (SIT) OPTION)

Here is one more exercise that has two signs. You halt at the first sign and cue your dog to sit and stay. Then you walk to the next sign (approximately fifteen feet away) and turn and face your dog. Call your dog to come and when he is about halfway to you, cue him to lie down (drop). After he is down, call him to come again, this time ending in a sit front. At your discretion, cue your dog to finish or forward either right or left.

If you are already training for the drop on recall (DOR) in competition obedience, the only difference here is that the distance is much shorter—only fifteen feet rather than the approximately forty feet you may be used to, and the judge does not signal you to "down your dog." You just have to get your hand signal/verbal cue out faster.

On average the drop on recall takes only a few days to train—sometimes just a few sessions. To train it, you break down the behavior into two different pieces; the stop and the drop.

The Stop

Use light colored and somewhat heavy treats for this so your dog can find them. Toss a treat about ten or more feet away and tell your dog to "get it." Have one treat in your signal hand and your clicker in the other hand. As he is coming back to you, put your hand up in a signal like a traffic cop—not wishy-washy, but forcefully, with a slight forward movement to your hand as if you were banging a wall with your hand and then with a slight "recoil" to your signal. (For some reason, this bouncing back of your hand makes all the difference.) When your dog stops (and 99 percent of all dogs do stop, perhaps because they are startled), click and toss him the treat from your hand. Be sure when you toss the treat that your hand movement is the same that you used to stop him (i.e., don't throw the treat underhand). It's really that simple. Play the game many times, clicking and treating each time your dog stops as if he's walked into a brick wall.

If your dog belongs to the one percentile of dogs that look at you blankly when you make your signal, don't despair—just do it this way: Put your hand up in the same way as described above, but toss the treat right at your dog. When he stops to find it, click (you are clicking the stop here). He'll get the treat, so you don't have to toss another one. You can get another repetition done from there—when he is done eating the treat you threw at him and he is coming back to you, just throw another one at him and repeat. Practice this many times until your dog is stopping when you raise your hand. Some dogs pick this up quickly and others take a longer time to understand what is expected of them. For this option, be sure to use treats that are heavy so your dog can hear them land.

The stop...

...and the drop.

Please train this exercise a lot. It may just save your dog's life one day. I have used this in the real world. One day, totally out of character, my dogs decided that running across the road was a really cool thing to do. I called them and they started to return to me. Only then did I see the car. I screamed and signaled the drop—and all three of them went down like stones. I reminded them to stay, and thankfully they did.

When you practice this for the real world, do not call your dog to you after he drops—you go to him, give him tons of treats, and then put the leash on or take him by the collar. The reason for this is if he were to decide to break the down/stay in anticipation of finishing the recall, he may still be in danger from whatever it was that scared you in the first place. You want your dog to stop, drop and *stay*.

The Drop

Now that your dog is stopping unbelievably fast, you can progress to the drop portion. Instructions for training the new drop signal are listed above (see APDT sign number 52). As your dog stops on cue, click and don't toss a treat. Keep your hand held high and ask your dog to down. If you have done your homework, this should happen pretty fast. If it doesn't, just keep your arm raised and repeat your verbal cue one more time and click and treat when he drops. Make sure you go to him to deliver the treat. Dropping a jackpot of treats between his front legs is the best way to help keep him "grounded" and to reinforce his position. If you toss a treat and miss, he is actually being reinforced for getting up and moving. You want to make it clear that the drop is what you want. After a few repetitions, your dog should be dropping like a stone.

The Rest

To train the balance of the exercise, once your dog is down, call him to you to sit front. Then you have your choice of which direction (right or left) and option (forward or finish) to do next. If you are in the Open level of competition obedience, don't forget which sport you are doing—the judge in Rally will not be cueing you at any point during this exercise.

Putting It All Together

Be sure that you also train your dog to do the entire exercise in a more formal way. Ask your dog to sit and stay, and then walk out fifteen feet. Turn and call your dog, and signal him to drop, then come, then finish.

BONUS EXERCISE: HALT/LEAVE DOG TURN AND DOWN

APDT ONLY #61

#62

LEVEL 2 BONUS

This sign is really a sort of drop on recall, without the recall. If you have worked your stop and drop cues, this will be a piece of cake for you and your dog won't creep forward on the down at a distance. Heel up to the first sign and have your dog sit. Walk to the second sign, face your dog and from there, ask him to down. You can use either a verbal or hand signal or both. Remember that if you use both, they have to be presented simultaneously, otherwise you will get points off for a double command. You then go back to him and the exercise ends when you are in heel position. You are allowed to say stay after he downs while you go back to him.

ENDING EXERCISES

BONUS EXERCISE: TURN/HALT/RETRIEVE/FINISH

LEVEL 3

This is a bonus exercise and is not included in course time. As with the other bonus exercises, before starting your run you must advise the judge whether or not you will be doing the bonus exercise. Once you commit to doing it, you are not allowed to change your mind. You hand the ring steward your retrieve object; this can be anything—a toy, dumbbell, glove, bumper, etc. As you are heeling to this bonus sign, the ring steward unobtrusively places the object on the floor approximately fifteen feet from the sign. This is done while your back is to the sign so that your dog doesn't see it. At the sign, you perform either an about U turn or an about right turn and halt. Your dog sits. You direct your dog to look at the object and then send the dog to pick it up and return to front position. Your dog must hold the object in his mouth until you ask him for it. You then do either a right or left finish at your own discretion.

Since APDT allows any type of item, it is best if you use an object your dog is already accustomed to retrieving. If your dog is very toy motivated, the hardest part of this exercise may be to get the sit as you do the about or right about turn. Just reward the sit heavily, and then as an added bonus for your dog, signal him to get the toy. When competing, you have to point to the toy so your dog knows it's there since it won't be thrown—the steward will have already placed it there beforehand.

Andrea indicating the retrieve
object to Quigley.

If your dog is used to bringing stuff to you but then drops the object, train him to do this correctly by back chaining. Train the "sit front with a toy in his mouth" first. Ask your dog to sit front and hand him your item. As soon as he takes it (providing he doesn't then stand or run off), click and treat.

Do this quite a few times until your dog is comfortable with sitting and holding the item for longer periods of time (just a few seconds longer each time). Once he is comfortable with that, you will also have to get the "give" on cue. Practice this as a separate behavior. If your dog is reluctant to give up his toy, you can use two of the same item, giving him the second one as soon as he gives you the one in his mouth.

As long as he is sitting nicely and giving when you ask, you can put the whole exercise together. Here are its components:

- your back to the retrieve object that the steward has placed down for you
- the turn and sit
- the point to the item
- the release to the item
- the pickup of the item
- the retrieve

- the sit front
- the give
- and, finally, the finish

I'll bet you didn't realize how many parts there were to this! At each step, be sure to randomly click and reinforce. That way each portion will remain strong and reliable.

Back chaining the retrieve. Beau has the dumbbell in his mouth while he sits in front position.

HONOR EXERCISE

AKC ONLY   #50

Honor

EXCELLENT LEVEL

In this exercise, you and your dog, on leash, do a stay in the ring while the next dog walks the course. You go to the station directly after completing your Excellent run. The judge designates whether your dog is to perform a sit/stay or a down/stay and also tells you at that time if you are to stand next to or in front

Please be aware that while *your* dog will be on leash, the other dog on the course will be *off leash*. Even though this exercise is in the Excellent level and trouble shouldn't happen, if you sense or see any possible conflict between the two dogs (and especially if the dog in the ring is paying no attention to his handler or is racing around the ring completely out of control), hightail it outta there! Forget the leg or even the title. Your dog will be on leash and thus unable to keep himself safe by running away. Call me a worrywart if you will, I don't mind. You owe it to your dog to keep him safe at all times. Many people know of or own dogs that were attacked while doing a group stay in competition obedience; in many cases, the dogs are now so afraid that they can no longer appear in the ring.

of your dog. The honor exercise must not be in the path of the dog and handler team that follows. Volunteer dogs will be used for both honoring the first dog in the class and for a course run-through when the last dog performs the honor exercise.

There is no time limit (as of this printing, although it is being discussed) for walking an AKC Rally course, so this may end up being a very long stay—anywhere from two to four or five minutes, or even more. Although, according to some judges, the longer times are not the norm, I like to train a long stay just in case. There is nothing magical or unique about training this behavior, aside from the amount of patience required to simply stand there. As many of you already know, stays can be boring with a capital B to train.

The honor exercise is a little easier to teach and execute than other stays because you are with your dog the entire time. You can, as in all the other exercises, talk to your dog, encouraging him to stay if he gets antsy.

Very simply, you use the heeling chart in Chapter 3 but you count seconds instead of steps. Just double the times and go on from there. Practice this both in front of and next to your dog, as well as the sit/stay and down/stay, because you want to be ready and prepared for all options.

RALLY AROUND

- There are lots of fun behaviors to train in this chapter! As you have seen, by breaking them down into tiny pieces, they aren't so scary anymore, are they?
- As with all of the behaviors listed in this book, be sure to practice these exercises in areas of low-level distractions at first, gradually adding distractions like those you would find at a trial.
- Be sure to practice in safe places so you can work off leash. Do not try to jump your dog while on leash—he can easily trip on the leash or you may inadvertently yank his neck.

chapter

◀ **8** ▶

POSITIVE SOLUTIONS
AND POSITIVE PROOFING

Teaching the behaviors listed in this book will be quite easy for some of you, depending on the prior training and experience you and your dog have had. I do understand that if you are a more novice handler, you may encounter some problems that you don't know how to fix. In this chapter I discuss common issues handlers and dogs run into that aren't covered in each specific sign's description. I draw upon issues I've had with my own dogs as well as those I've seen with my students' dogs (and I even polled some judges). The problems all have one thing in common. Can you guess what it is? The answer is waiting for you at the end of the chapter.

Once you start putting together some practice courses, you will set them up so that the signs are slightly to the right of where your path will be. Most likely, the only sign that will be directly in your path will be the moving side step right (taught in Chapter 5).

Be aware that your dog may be distracted by the signs themselves the first time he sees them. Let him roam around and sniff them. You may also find that you get distracted by them as well, so be sure you practice!

POSITIVE SOLUTIONS

PROBLEM   Let's say you have some pretty decent heeling going on for approximately fifteen to twenty steps and/or approximately forty-five to sixty seconds. Every now and then, however, your dog looks or moves away.

SOLUTION   Every time your dog looks away, say "Ha!" and run in the opposite direction. Be careful to keep the leash loose so as not to pop him or, better yet, do this off leash if you are in a safe area. As soon as he catches up, heel a few more steps, click and then heavily reinforce him. Usually after you do this a few times, your dog will be heavily glued to you. Stay away from clicking the instant he gets back to you—otherwise he will think you are rewarding him for losing focus.

PROBLEM   Every time you give your dog a treat, he goes off into la-la land for a few seconds or a few steps and then comes back to you.

SOLUTION   You are most likely too predictable in how you reinforce and what you are seeing here is called "scalloping." That means you are probably clicking and feeding at the same number of steps or seconds, and feeding the same number of treats each time (many people get stuck on only feeding the same old one treat each time) and not using other types of reinforcers. To correct this, become more unpredictable in how and when you reinforce. Utilize the heeling chart in Chapter 3 to help you become more variable in your schedule of reinforcement.

PROBLEM   Your dog continues to forge when heeling.

SOLUTION   One of the best cures I have found for a forging problem is to start with one step of heeling. Click and treat for your dog remaining in heel position, but feed the treat in a slightly different manner. Have the treat in your left hand, but reach both hands back behind you as if you are taking the treat out of your right hand. Then feed in position. Repeat this dozens of times. Gradually do two steps of heeling, then three, and so on.

My second favorite way to help with this problem is the "follow my eyes" game to keep your dog in position. With your head still pointing straight, lock eyes with your dog and then look where you want him to be. (Try very hard not to turn your head to the left—trust me, he can see your eyes. If he can't, a trip to the groomer for him is in order, or you need to pull your own hair back.) Ninety-nine percent of all dogs will hesitate or actually drop back to heel position. Once your dog hesitates

Reaching behind to get the treat.

even for a split second, click and treat that pause. Continue to practice both of these methods—pretending you are grabbing the treat from behind you and using your eyes to place him in proper position—and you should start to see a big difference.

PROBLEM Your dog continues to lag.

SOLUTION Make sure you aren't cheer-leading him to "hurry, hurry!" This will only reinforce him for lagging in the first place. Your happy voice should happen *when* he is in perfect heel position, not to *get* him into perfect heel position. For a lagging dog, I like to make sure he can't lag in the first place, which means you have to slow down until he is no longer lagging. Gradually, once his confidence builds, you can go slightly faster. You can click for the proper position and instead of feeding him in heel position, toss the treat ahead about ninety-five percent of the time.

PROBLEM Your dog isn't coming in straight on the call front/recall.

SOLUTION Go back and play the "front" game in Chapter 2. You can also borrow the "follow my eyes" game from the solution above. As your dog is coming to you, lock eyes with him and draw your eyes directly to front position. Don't move your head—just your eyes. You should start to see a dog that is coming in straighter.

PROBLEM You take your dog in the ring and he won't stop sniffing.

SOLUTION You need to do more attention work with distractions present and do more match shows. You also need to make sure that *you* aren't nervous, because that tension will go right down the leash to your dog. There is a book reference for "ring nerves" in Appendix 3 that you may find helpful. What you are most likely seeing with excessive sniffing or inattention is a stressed dog, trying to calm you or himself down, or a dog that hasn't been trained enough in working around distractions. The more you let this behavior go on, the more stressed you will become and the more your dog will ignore you.

If you have gone through at least half of the course with no attention from your dog, I would recommend turning to the judge and asking, "May I please be excused?" I don't know any judge who will refuse your request. We all have done this at one time or another, so try not to feel humiliated—just chalk it up to your dog needing more training.

PROBLEM Your dog loses focus during training.

SOLUTION Try really hard not to drill your dog. I have Border Collies and I don't drill them even though I know they can handle it. Four to five repetitions of any given exercise is more than enough for one session. Make it fun for your dog and be unpredictable in how you reinforce. You may know some dogs that seem to be able to focus for longer periods of time than your dog, but you must work with the dog you have, rather than against him by pretending he is something he's not. I train many breeds of dogs that are not traditional obedience types, some with behavioral problems as well, and almost without exception, they can be taught to have beautiful focus and precision.

I know I have mentioned being unpredictable many, many times in this book. I'll give you a concrete example of my own experience and how it changed my entire outlook on training. I thought one of my dogs, Beau, was ready to show in Novice competition obedience. I entered him in about five trials; each time, he performed worse and worse, giving me less and less attention. He was great comic relief for the crowd, as I was heeling by myself and he was off in a corner rolling around in the grass, hugely enjoying himself. Rather than continuing to look ridiculous, I stopped entering him and sat back and thought about my training. I realized I was incredibly boring and incredibly predictable in how I rewarded him. I started to be fun—offering play, tug, fetch, swimming, scads of treats, sniffing the treat, etc. His training in private became supercharged and his scores in the ring went from a consistent zero to being consistently above 195. At the trial where he earned his second CD title (AKC and ASCA) he finished up with a 198 (out of a possible 200) and High in Trial, with all but one leg being a placement. For his first Open leg, he earned a 199! His Rally scores have been very high as well—averaging between 197 and 203. Ah! Behold the power of fun!

REWARDS

Many people find teaching heeling to be very boring and subsequently their dogs feel the same way. If you make the whole process fun for your dog, you will find it enjoyable yourself. There are a million things you can use to reward your dog. Be creative, be different each time and try to stay out of a rut. Using the short list from Chapter 2, possible reinforcers other than food can be:

- Petting softly
- Petting roughly (if your dog enjoys this)
- Letting your dog sniff the treat (no eating!)
- Playing tug (always let him win)
- Tossing a toy
- Running around and encouraging him to chase you ("tag, you're it" game)
- Letting your dog play with a doggie pal
- Teasing him with a toy (no playing!)
- Clapping and cheering
- Letting him sniff the ground
- Tossing the treats up in the air while making silly noises
- Having your dog do some favorite pet tricks
- Giving him water (to drink)
- Letting him play in water
- Tossing grass and snow in the air

You don't have to stop there—whatever floats your dog's boat can be used. You can set up your sessions ahead of time; decide what reinforcers you will use and how often you will reward your dog. Be sure to change the list for each training session to keep it fresh and fun for both of you.

SESSIONS

Setting up the mix of behaviors is important as well. Practicing only one or two things all of the time is boring for both you and your dog. A typical fifteen-minute training session can look like this:

- Heel using Morgan Spector's chart for two levels, using three different reinforcers
- Four "come up/sits" using food

- Three repetitions of jumping using toys and play as the reward
- One retrieve with ten treats as the reward
- Two "call front/finish left," one time rewarding with a few treats tossed in the air and one time with playing "tag, you're it"
- Two moving stands using sniffing the treat as one reward and sniffing the ground as the second reward
- Working on "mine" (food bowl exercise) for about four minutes with tons of treats and play as the reward
- One halt/sit/walk around with the reward being soft petting
- Teaching a pet trick such as roll over or spin, using food as the reward

As you can see, I mixed up all of the Rally levels (and added a pet trick) and didn't just list behaviors in level one. Many competition obedience trainers will train all levels, not just one at a time. Some of the more complicated behaviors take longer to train, so you may as well start now!

A fun way to help you decide what behaviors to practice and what reinforcers to use would be to print out all of the behaviors you want to work on and cut them into strips and place them in a box. Then write down all of the things your dog likes on strips of paper and place them in a different box. For each training session, pick a few slips out of each box and voilà! Instant training session! This way, every time you practice, it will be something new and creative.

PROOFING

Once you have gotten to a certain level of proficiency in heeling (and in each of the behaviors listed in this book), there are different ways to positively "proof" your dog. Positive proofing does not mean setting the dog up to be wrong so that you can then "correct" him but, instead, presenting some distractions (little ones at first and at a big distance) and heavily reinforcing your dog for ignoring them and, in fact, making it *fun* for him to ignore them and make the right choice. If he does get distracted, just decrease the distance, duration or intensity of the distraction back to the level in which he was successful. Then gradually go back to increasing the distraction until he is actively avoiding it.

Proofing is really all about your dog's solid attention to you and solid name and come response, and your own mastery of the "art" of knowing when to make a step easier for your dog to understand. When you are proofing something new for the first time and your dog gets distracted, just stand still and wait. Even if it takes five minutes for his attention to come back to you, reward him anyway. If you don't, the next time he won't even bother trying to make the effort.

PROBLEM   Your dog is great at home and completely inattentive anywhere else, and you feel embarrassed and like all your training was for naught.

SOLUTION   Well...as I mentioned in Chapter 2 and elsewhere, you must train all of the behaviors in many places. If you practice only in a few familiar places that have the same types of distractions, then your dog may fall apart in new locations or at trials. Dogs are funny creatures—what they learn in one location remains in that location. If you want your dog to perform in new places the way he performs at home, you must help him generalize those behaviors by going to many different places and experiencing many different types of distractions. Once he can perform with consistency in all settings, then you can say he has fully generalized the behavior.

DISTRACTIONS

There are millions of things to train and proof your dog around. The most common ones are: other dogs, barking dogs, lunging dogs, all different types of people (with beards, hats, umbrellas), a stranger following you around with a clipboard (i.e., the judge), kids running around screaming (although at show sites this is frowned upon big time, it does occasionally happen), strollers, firecrackers, thunder, trains, big trucks, gunshots, sirens, honking cars, papers and tents flying around because a windstorm suddenly blew in, rain, loudspeakers, people yelling, loose dogs, echoes in buildings, different types of flooring (grass, uneven footing, mats), ringside issues (people/dogs/kids that are too close, eating food, and playing with their own dogs ringside with tug or squeaky toys), tape or chalk on the floor, balloons, flower pots, mirrors, reflections from the sun coming from windows and the Rally signs themselves.

While it may be impossible to proof for everything that rolls down the pike, if you can build to a good level of proficiency with most of them, that training will most likely see you through the new distractions.

THE LIAR'S GAME

A typical distraction "game" you can play is something I call the "liar's" game. Basically, you want to teach your dog that everyone else in the world is a liar and *you always* pay off. The first section uses the game when practicing for the recall (come) and the second section when practicing for heeling.

Recall—Part One

1. Have someone hold your dog.
2. Have a second person (the "liar") stand in the middle of the room or yard with some food or toys. Start with something of relatively low value to the dog. We want to set him up for success!
3. You go across the room or yard.
4. Call your dog to come.
5. The liar tries to gently distract the dog. The liar does not let the dog have the goodies or give the dog eye contact.
6. Do not repeat your cue—just wait.
7. When the dog comes to you, click and treat with a huge jackpot.
8. Repeat a bunch of times until the dog is actively avoiding the liar.

Recall—Part Two

➡ Increase the number of the distractions—add a dog (only if both dogs are dog-friendly!), making sure that your dog cannot get to the "distraction" dog. When your dog comes to you, you can click and give a huge jackpot and then as an additional bonus prize, you can let both dogs play.

➡ Increase the value of the objects that the liar has, making sure that your jackpots rise in value also.

➡ Add some additional liars and have a few people trying to distract the dog away from his mission of coming to you.

Warning on item 3—do not use family members as liars! Beyond Rally, it is important that your dog respond to all family members.

DISTRACTION HEELING

This is very similar to the game as played above. The only difference is that you heel around the liar—you do not call your dog. You just keep heeling while the liar continues to try to distract your dog. If your dog goes to the liar, you keep walking. When your dog does come within a foot of you, click and treat, then keep heeling. Every time your dog comes close to you, click and treat. Vary the amounts of the jackpots, and if you want, you can add in a quick game of tug or other types of play. Again, start out with easy distractions (such as a whisper of "puppy, puppy" with fingers wiggling) to set the dog up for success and gradually increase the very high level of the distractions, such as chasing after the dog with hand outstretched, holding an open peanut butter jar (yes, I have done this!). Add in lots of pace and direction changes to keep your dog's interest.

RALLY AROUND

- Set your dog up to succeed, and please don't get angry with him if he gets distracted—he will make mistakes, but this training is all about teaching him that the distractions are nothing, that you are the most wonderful, fun thing around!
- Make it fun for your dog to be riveted on you and he will be.

Answer to the question at the start of this chapter: *Attention!*

◀ 9 ▶

IT'S ALL IN THE DETAILS

Every sport has its own many nuances, and Rally is no different. Major differences in judging criteria are not discussed in this book because there are too many variations between the two venues. However, some things are common to both APDT and AKC and also relate to competing in general. I remember how stupid I felt when I was just starting to compete—I wish I had had a chapter like this back then.

PREMIUMS AND REGISTRATION FORMS

The premium is the entry form. Before you enter your dog in an actual trial, you will need to make sure your dog is registered with the AKC and/or APDT. Remember, APDT Rally accepts mixed breed dogs but AKC Rally only accepts registered purebred dogs of breeds recognized by the AKC. There are times when you may not have actual papers on your purebred dog (if, for instance, you rescued him); you can, however, get what is called an ILP number for him. ILP stands for Indefinite Listing Privileges. With that designation, you are allowed to show your paperless, purebred dog in AKC trials.

APDT dog registry form. You must register with the APDT
and get a registration number before entering a trial.

Rally Obedience
for All Dogs

Registration Form

You must register your dog(s) with APDT Rally in order to
compete with them in APDT Rally Trials and earn APDT
Rally legs and titles.

Complete a separate registration form for each team
you are registering. **Please print clearly or type –**
this information will appear on all RallyO records.
Registration confirmation will be emailed to you.
If you do not have email, it will be sent via US mail.
Please allow 2-4 weeks for processing.

Dog's Name: _____

Dog's Date of Birth (approximate if unknown): _____

Breed(s) (best approximation if unknown): _____

Owner's/Co-owner's Name(s): _____

Address: _____

_____

Telephone: _____ **Email:** _____

Fees:
Rally Registration ....$ 35.00

Less Spay/Neuter Discount (**enclose proof**), <$10> .... _____

Less APDT Member Discount
(Member Number/Expiration Date _____), <$10> .... _____

                    TOTAL... _____

PAYMENT INFORMATION

Enclosed is a check (payable to APDT in US funds drawn on U.S. banking institutions, International Postal
Money Orders in U.S. funds, or credit cards) $_____ Charge my credit card $ _____

Circle one: Visa   MasterCard   American Express

Account # _____ Expiration Date_____

Cardholder Name _____

Signature of Cardholder _____

Mail to: *APDT Rally*
31 Revere Ave., Maplewood NJ 07040

Complete APDT Rally Rules and Eligibility Information, Registration Form, Judge and Rally
Representative Information is available on the APDT website at www.apdt.com/rallyo/index.htm.

For office use only

Date Rec'd: _____ Amount Rec'd: _____ Initials: _____ Registration #: _____
APDT RallyO Dog/Handler Team Registration Form
September 24, 2003

AKC registration form (page 1). As with APDT, you must have a registration number before entering a trial.

AKC registration form (page 2).

Dog Registration Application

AF2AJ

AMERICAN KENNEL CLUB

SA00000002

Litter Owner Information — Please check one box and sign above your preprinted name(s)

☐ I (we) still own this dog and apply for registration and to have ownership recorded in my (our) name(s).

☐ I (we) transferred this dog **directly** to the owner(s) listed in the New Owner(s) section below.

I (we) certify by my (our) signature(s) that all the information appearing on this application is correct and that I (we) am (are) in good standing with the American Kennel Club. I (WE) AGREE THAT ANY CAUSE OF ACTION, CONTROVERSY OR CLAIM ARISING OUT OF OR RELATED TO THIS REGISTRATION OR AS TO THE CONSTRUCTION, INTERPRETATION AND EFFECT OF THIS AGREEMENT SHALL BE SETTLED BY ARBITRATION PURSUANT TO THE APPLICABLE RULES OF THE AMERICAN ARBITRATION ASSOCIATION. HOWEVER, PRIOR TO ARBITRATION ALL APPLICABLE AKC BYLAWS, RULES, REGULATIONS AND PROCEDURES MUST FIRST BE FOLLOWED AS SET FORTH IN THE AKC CHARTER AND BYLAWS, RULES, REGULATIONS, PUBLISHED POLICIES AND GUIDELINES.

SAMPLE

JOHN DOE

New Owner(s) Information — PLEASE PRINT

Date of Transfer: ☐☐-☐☐-☐☐☐☐
Month   Day   Year

New Owner's First Name _____ New Owner's Last Name _____

Mailing Address _____

City _____ State ☐☐ ZIP code + 4 ☐☐☐☐☐-☐☐☐☐

☐☐☐-☐☐☐-☐☐☐☐
Telephone Number   Email Address _____

New Co-Owner's First Name _____ New Co-Owner's Last Name _____

Mailing Address _____

City _____ State ☐☐ ZIP code + 4 ☐☐☐☐☐-☐☐☐☐

☐☐☐-☐☐☐-☐☐☐☐
Telephone Number   Email Address _____

New Owner(s)—Read and sign below

I (we) apply to the American Kennel Club to have a Registration Certificate for this dog issued in my (our) name(s). I (we) certify that I (we) acquired this dog directly on the date stated above from the Litter Owner(s) and if applicable, that I (we) have complete written authority from the other owner(s) to submit this application to register this dog in all our names. I (we) understand that upon request I (we) will be required to provide to the AKC any such written authorization. I (we) agree to abide by all rules and regulations of the American Kennel Club. I (we) understand that if the Limited box on the Dog Registration Application has been darkened completely by the Litter Owner(s), I (we) will receive a Limited Registration Certificate. I (WE) AGREE THAT ANY CAUSE OF ACTION, CONTROVERSY OR CLAIM ARISING OUT OF OR RELATED TO THIS REGISTRATION OR AS TO THE CONSTRUCTION, INTERPRETATION AND EFFECT OF THIS AGREEMENT SHALL BE SETTLED BY ARBITRATION PURSUANT TO THE APPLICABLE RULES OF THE AMERICAN ARBITRATION ASSOCIATION. HOWEVER, PRIOR TO ARBITRATION ALL APPLICABLE AKC BYLAWS, RULES, REGULATIONS AND PROCEDURES MUST FIRST BE FOLLOWED AS SET FORTH IN THE AKC CHARTER AND BYLAWS, RULES, REGULATIONS, PUBLISHED POLICIES AND GUIDELINES.

New Owner's Signature _____ New Co-Owner's Signature _____

Instructions, Requirements, and General Information

Supplemental Transfer Instructions	If you did not acquire this dog directly from the litter owner(s), you must include a Supplemental Transfer Statement with fee for *each* intermediate transfer with this application. Multiply the number of Supplemental Transfer Statements by the amount shown under Additional Fees on page 1 of this application and include this amount in the total payment. **Note:** This form is available on our Web site: www.akc.org.
Mailing Address	Send this form and all appropriate fees to: The American Kennel Club, P.O. Box 37902, Raleigh, NC 27627-7902
Additional Requirements	If there are more than two New Owners, contact the AKC for an Additional Signature form. **Note:** This form is available on our Web site: www.akc.org.
Authorizations	Signatures of persons other than the owners will be accepted only if a properly completed authorization form has been filed with the AKC. **Note:** These forms are available on our Web site: www.akc.org.
Assistance	Email AKC at info@akc.org or call 919-233-9767 to speak to an AKC Customer Service Representative, Monday — Friday, 8:30 AM — 5:00 PM. Information about the registration process and downloadable forms are available on our Web site: www.akc.org.

ADREG2 (9405)

AKC premium (page 1).

OFFICIAL AMERICAN KENNEL CLUB ENTRY FORM

I ENCLOSE $ ....for entry fees

IMPORTANT-Read Carefully Instructions on Reverse Side Before Filling Out. Numbers in the boxes indicate sections of the instructions relevant to the information needed in that box (PLEASE PRINT)

BREED	VARIETY 1		SEX
DOG 2 3 SHOW CLASS		CLASS 3 DIVISION Weight, color, etc.	
ADDITIONAL CLASSES	OBEDIENCE CLASS	RALLY CLASS (Jump Height)	JR. SHOWMANSHIP CLASS
NAME OF (See Back) JUNIOR HANDLER (if any)			JR. HANDLER NUMBER

FULL
NAME
OF DOG

Enter number here

☐ AKC REG NO. ☐ AKC LITTER NO. ☐ ILP NO. ☐ FOREIGN REG NO & COUNTRY	DATE OF BIRTH
	PLACE OF BIRTH ☐USA ☐ Canada ☐ Foreign

BREEDER

SIRE

DAM

ACTUAL OWNER(S)_____
4   (Please Print)

OWNER'S ADDRESS _____

CITY_____ STATE _____ ZIP _____

NAME OF OWNER'S AGENT
(IF ANY) AT THE SHOW _____

I CERTIFY that I am the actual owner of the dog, or that I am the duly authorized agent of the actual owner whose name I have entered above. In consideration of the acceptance of this entry, I (we) agree to abide by the rules and regulations of The American Kennel Club in effect at the time of this event, and by any additional rules and regulations appearing in the premium list for this event, and further agree to be bound by the "Agreement" printed on the reverse side of this entry form. I (we) certify and represent that the dog entered is not a hazard to persons or other dogs. This entry is submitted for acceptance on the foregoing representation and Agreement. I (we) agree to conduct myself (ourselves) in accordance with all such Rules and Regulations (including all provisions applying to discipline) and to abide by any decisions made in accord with them.

■ SIGNATURE of owner or his agent
duly authorized to make this entry _____

TELEPHONE# _____

E-MAIL Address (An acknowledgment or receipt of entry may be sent to this e-mail address):

| | | | | | | | | | | | | | | | | | | | | | | | | | | | | | | | | | |

AEN999 (11/04)

AKC premium (page 2).

AGREEMENT

I (we) agree that the club holding this event has the right to refuse this entry for cause which the club shall deem sufficient. In consideration of the acceptance of this entry and of the holding of this event and of the opportunity to have the dog judged and to win prizes, ribbons, or trophies, I (we) agree to hold the AKC, the event-giving club, their members, directors, governors, officers, agents, superintendents or event secretary and the owner and/or lessor of the premises and any provider of services that are necessary to hold this event and any employees or volunteers of the aforementioned parties, and any AKC approved judge, judging at this event, harmless from any claim for loss or injury which may be alleged to have been caused directly or indirectly to any person or thing by the act of this dog while in or about the event premises or grounds or near any entrance thereto, and I (we) personally assume all responsibility and liability for any such claim; and I (we) further agree to hold the aforementioned parties harmless from any claim for loss, injury or damage to this dog.

Additionally, I (we) hereby assume the sole responsibility for and agree to indemnify, defend and save the aforementioned parties harmless from any and all loss and expense (including legal fees) by reason of the liability imposed by law upon any of the aforementioned parties for damage because of bodily injuries, including death at any time resulting therefrom, sustained by any person or persons, including myself (ourselves), or on account of damage to property, arising out of or in consequence of my (our) participation in this event, however such, injuries, death or property damage may be caused, and whether or not the same may have been caused or may be alleged to have been caused by the negligence of the aforementioned parties or any of their employees, agents, or any other persons. **I (WE) AGREE THAT ANY CAUSE OF ACTION, CONTROVERSY OR CLAIM ARISING OUT OF OR RELATED TO THE ENTRY, EXHIBITION OR ATTENDANCE AT THE EVENT BETWEEN THE AKC AND THE EVENT-GIVING CLUB (UNLESS OTHERWISE STATED IN ITS PREMIUM LIST) AND MYSELF (OURSELVES) OR AS TO THE CONSTRUCTION, INTERPRETATION AND EFFECT OF THIS AGREEMENT SHALL BE SETTLED BY ARBITRATION PURSUANT TO THE APPLICABLE RULES OF THE AMERICAN ARBITRATION ASSOCIATION. HOWEVER, PRIOR TO ARBITRATION ALL APPLICABLE AKC BYLAWS, RULES, REGULATIONS AND PROCEDURES MUST FIRST BE FOLLOWED AS SET FORTH IN THE AKC CHARTER AND BYLAWS, RULES, REGULATIONS, PUBLISHED POLICIES AND GUIDELINES.**

INSTRUCTIONS

1. (Variety) if you are entering a dog of breed in which there are varieties for show purposes, please designate the particular variety you are entering, i.e., Cocker Spaniel (solid color black, ASCOB, parti-color), Beagles (not exceeding 13 in., over 13 in. but not exceeding 15 in.), Dachshunds (longhaired, smooth, wirehaired), Collies (rough, smooth), Bull Terriers (colored, white), Manchester Terriers (standard, toy), Chihuahuas (smooth coat, long coat), English Toy Spaniels (King Charles and Ruby, Blenheim and Prince Charles), Poodles (toy, miniature, standard).

2. The following categories of dogs may be entered and shown in Best of Breed competition: Dogs that are Champions of Record and dogs which, according to their owners' records, have completed the requirements for a championship, but whose championships are unconfirmed. The showing of unconfirmed Champions in Best of Breed competition is limited to a period of 90 days from the date of the show where the dog completed the requirements for a championship.

3. (Event Class) Consult the classification in this premium list. If the event class in which you are entering your dog is divided, then, in addition to designating the class, specify the particular division of the class in which you are entering your dog, i.e, age division, color division, weight division.

4. A dog must be entered in the name of the person who actually owned it at the time entries for an event closed. If a registered dog has been acquired by a new owner it must be entered in the name of its new owner in any event for which entries closed after the date of acquirement, regardless of whether the new owner has received the registration certificate indicating that the dog is recorded in his name. State on entry form whether transfer application has been mailed to the AKC. (For complete rules, refer to Chapter 11, Section 3.)

If this entry is for Junior Showmanship, please give the following information:

JUNIOR SHOWMANSHIP   JR.'S DATE OF BIRTH_____

AKC JUNIOR HANDLER NUMBER ☐☐☐☐☐☐☐☐☐☐☐☐

The above number MUST be included. Should you not have your Junior Handler number, this may be obtained from the American Kennel Club. Phone: (919) 816-3776.

By signing the entry form I (we) certify that the Junior Showman does not now, and will not at any time, act as an agent/handler for pay while continuing to compete in Junior Showmanship.

ADDRESS _____

CITY _____ STATE _____ ZIP _____

▪ If Junior Handler is not the owner of the dog identified on the face of this form, what is the relationship of the Junior Handler to the Owner?

_____

AEN999 (11/04)

APDT premium.

OFFICIAL ENTRY FORM

DOG INFORMATION

Reg. Name:			Rally Registration#:	
Call Name:			Height at Withers:	
Will be using food:	YES	NO	Circle *ALL* APDT Rally Titles: Level 1	Level 2
Date of Birth:			Breed:	
* Dog must have APDT Rally-O registration number				

OWNER/HANDLER INFORMATION

Name:			
Address:			
City:		State:	Zip:
Phone:	(day) (evening)	E-mail:	
Handler's Name (must be member of immediate family):			

Entries accepted on a first-come-first served basis. Confirmations will be sent out after entries have closed. Those wishing earlier notification that their entry has been accepted should enclose a self-addressed, stamped post card with their entry.

TRIAL ENTRY AND FEE INFORMATION (CHECK CHOICES)
Times are approximate

Trial 1 - $20 8:30 AM (Level 1)	Trial 2 - $20 9:30 AM (Level 1)	Trial 1 - $20 10:30 AM (Level 2)	Trial 2 - $20 11:30 AM (Level 2)	Trial 1 - $20 12:30 PM (Level 3)	Trial 2 - $20 1:30 PM (Level 3)

ENTRY FEES SUBMITTED

Total Trial Entry Fees (	$

This entry is not valid unless the agreement on the reverse side of this form has been **completed, signed, and dated.** *In order to be valid, entries must also be received with correct fees by the closing date at the address provided above. Entries will be accepted by overnight mail only if the signature requirement has been waived.*

MATCH SHOWS

A match show is a practice dog show. This allows you to get your dog (and you) used to the ring as well as to typical show distractions before actually entering into a trial. If you have never competed before, I highly recommend doing quite a few matches so that both you and your dog are comfortable with the ring setting—its sights, sounds and etiquette. Matches are less expensive than real trials; depending on where you live, they usually run about $5.00 to $9.00 per entry, versus the $20.00 to $25.00 for a show.

You can generally find listings of Rally match shows (and trials) in a few places: on the APDT and AKC websites, or if you live on the East Coast, in a publication called the *Match Show Bulletin* that lists all sorts of matches, shows, seminars, etc.

SCORING

In APDT, the maximum score for a performance you can get is a 200. Each level has an optional bonus exercise for a maximum point value of 10 points. Thus, effective January 1, 2006, scores of up to 210 are possible in APDT Rally. Only scores of 170 or above are qualifying scores. In AKC, score maximum is 100, and qualifying scores are 70 or above. Information on the actual scoring of each exercise can be found on the respective websites for each venue.

ETIQUETTE

Like any sport, Rally has certain etiquette do's and don'ts.

DO'S

➡ Make sure you are well versed on scoring policies for each venue. You can find that information on their websites.

➡ Pick up your number when you arrive at the show site. In APDT if you need a special alteration of the course (e.g., if you have an old, arthritic, blind or deaf dog), you must talk to the host club ahead of time and fill out a form. The judge may approve or disapprove the modification—there is no guarantee it will be approved. See *Special Consideration* below for more information on this matter.

USING FOOD IN APDT RALLY

- You cannot hold any food in your hand or in your mouth. No fanny packs are allowed in APDT, so make sure the food is in your pocket.

- You cannot drop any food on the course, so make darn sure the reward lands in your dog's mouth. Otherwise you will get three points off for each treat dropped.

- Food may be used as a reward only *after* an exercise is completed and only *before* you step off to go to the next sign and only as long as it doesn't impede the forward movement of your dog.

- When giving hand signals, make sure it doesn't look like you are luring with food—otherwise the judge may take points off or you may NQ.

- The armband/number goes on your left arm. Rubber bands are usually supplied to hold them in place.

- Arrive early to get yourself and your dog acclimated to the site. I always walk my dog around the outside of the ring to get him used to the sights and smells beforehand. If you do this, it must be before the show starts and when there are no dogs in the ring.

- Make sure you potty your dog before going into the ring. If your dog eliminates in the ring, you will be asked to leave.

- Breathe.

- Be ready when your number is called. You will not endear yourself to the judge or fellow competitors if they are kept waiting.

- If you find yourself boxed in and are afraid of other (or your own) dogs' reactions, utilize the Rally moves you just learned! The call front works wonders, as does the moving side step right and the about turn.

- Breathe.

- Be sure to use the fully allotted time to walk the course. Try to avoid handler errors.

- If you have any questions for the judge, don't be shy—ask! That is why they have a judge's meeting before the runs start.

- When it is your turn to go into the ring, heel your dog to the ring rather than letting him sniff and possibly get into trouble.

- Breathe.
- Keep your ears open for the ring steward to announce the run order: "Cody on the line [get to the ring now!], Shadow on deck [due in after Cody], Beau in the hole [third dog in]."
- When it is your turn to enter the ring, wait at the ring gate for the judge to invite you in.

DON'TS

- When walking your dog around the outside of the ring, don't allow him to urinate or defecate next to or on the ring gates.
- Don't crowd or allow your dog to sniff other dogs or let other dogs crowd or sniff your dog (I stay far away from the other dogs—I never assume the other dogs are "nice.")
- Don't play with your dog right outside of the ring—it will distract the working dog and is very poor etiquette.

RING SAVVY

For both venues you will get a course map and you will be allowed to walk the course before judging starts. If you make a mistake on an exercise and realize it, most of the time it will behoove you to go back and do it again. That way you will only get a few points off rather than an NQ (non-qualify). The only time you don't want to do a "do over" is if your dog is slightly crooked on a sit, front or finish. That would only be one point off and if you redo it, you will get more points off than you would have lost.

Be sure that you give your dog enough room to work around the signs. If he (or you) knocks over a sign, points are taken off.

EQUIPMENT

Equipment is easily and inexpensively purchased from J&J Dog Supplies (see Appendix 3). You can also go to each venue's website and print the signs on your own computer and mount them on sturdy cardboard.

APPROPRIATE DRESS

While there is no dress code for dog shows, you will want to look your best. You have put in a great deal of training to get to this point and you want to show off as a team with your well-groomed dog. A clean shirt or sweater, long pants (jeans are okay as long as they are neat) and sneakers or shoes are preferred over sloppy T-shirts, torn jeans, shorts, stained clothing and sandals. Your hair should be neat. You may not wear any shirts or sweaters that have any kind of club or school logo on them. You can, however, wear shirts or sweaters with breed pictures.

My own personal preference is to stay away from overly trendy clothing. I like to dress so that my clothing either matches or complements the coloring of my dog.

CUES

In APDT, if you want to use both hand and verbal cues, you must give them simultaneously. Otherwise, the later cue will be judged as a second cue to your dog and you will get points off. For instance, if you verbally ask your dog to sit and he hesitates and you then either say "sit" again or use a hand signal, you will have points deducted. If you are uncertain as to whether your dog will respond, by all means use both cues at the same time. If you are heeling and you use the word "heel," you are allowed to use *different* words to continue to encourage him if he gets distracted. "Let's go," "with me," "right here, poochie woochie" are all allowed, but "heel," "heel," "heel" is not allowed.

In AKC, you are allowed to use any verbal encouragement whatsoever and may repeat the same cues numerous times with no points off.

SPECIAL CONSIDERATION

APDT permits exercises to be modified for physically challenged/disabled dogs and/or handlers. This will allow for your dog's slower sits or response time to not be judged against you. If you need to touch your dog to communicate, you are allowed to do so. Your dog may also need a lower jump height. You must inform the host club ahead of time (*before* judging starts), and they will give you a form to fill out to give to the judge. The judge has the right to approve or disapprove any modification. If you have a slower response time yourself, you can also inform the judge ahead of time.

RALLY AROUND

- Be sure you are well versed in the rules before entering a trial.
- Ask the judge any questions you may have before judging starts.
- Breathe.
- **Have fun!**

◄ 1 ►

RALLY TITLES

If you are new to showing, be prepared to get a little confused about title requirements. Read through the following criteria, but don't panic if you feel it is too much information and your head starts to spin. Just train the behaviors you need and reference the following only on an "as needed" basis. Once you become more comfortable and confident and have your first title (either level 1 in APDT or Novice in AKC) this will all start to make perfect sense.

APDT TITLE REQUIREMENTS

LEVEL 1 TITLE

- ➤ Three qualifying scores of 170 or better, earned under two different judges, in the A class are required.
- ➤ The Rally Level 1 title is designated as RL1 and appears after the dog's name.

LEVEL 2 TITLE

- ➤ Three qualifying scores of 170 or better, earned under two different judges, in the A class are required.
- ➤ The Rally Level 2 title is designated as RL2 and appears after the dog's name.

LEVEL 3 TITLE

- ➤ Three qualifying scores of 170 or better, earned under two different judges, in the A class are required.
- ➤ The Rally Level 3 title is designated as RL3 and appears after the dog's name.

CHAMPIONSHIP TITLES

Once a team has earned a Level title, they may continue to compete at that level in the B class for Championship titles. The Championship title designations appear before the dog's name.

There are a few championship titles in APDT that you can work toward.

INDIVIDUAL LEVEL CHAMPIONSHIP TITLES

- ✦ Ten qualifying scores of 170 or higher are required to earn an Individual Level.
- ✦ These are designated as RL1X for Level 1, RL2X for Level 2 and RL3X for Level 3.
- ✦ Teams may continue to compete after the first ten qualifying scores have been earned. For each set of ten qualifying scores earned after the initial ten qualifying scores, the designation will be changed to RL1X2, RL1X3, RL1X4, and so on for Level 1; RL2X2, RL2X3, RL2X4, for Level 2; and RL3X2, RL3X3, RL3X4, for Level 3.
- ✦ Scores that also qualify for Combined Level Championship Titles will be credited toward those titles at the same time.

COMBINED LEVEL CHAMPIONSHIP TITLES

There are four Combined Level Championship Titles:

ARCH	APDT Rally Champion
ARCHX	APDT Rally Champion Excellent
ARCHEX	APDT Rally Champion Extraordinaire
ARCHMX	APDT Rally Master Champion

ARCH Championship Title—Any dog/handler team that has earned an APDT Rally Level 1 (RL1) and a Level 2 (RL2) title becomes eligible to begin qualifying for the APDT Rally Champion Title. To earn this title, the team must meet these requirements.

You must accumulate 100 Championship Title points in B classes. At least 30 of these must be earned in the Rally level 1 class and 30 from the Rally level 2 class. The remaining 40 points may be earned in either level. Championship Title points are earned in the Rally classes according to the following table (anything above a 200 score reflects how you scored on the bonus exercises):

Qualifying Score	Points Earned
191	1
192	2
193	3
194	4
195	5
196	6
197	7
198	8
199	9
200	10
201	11
202	12
203	13
204	14
205	15
206	16
207	17
208	18
209	18
210	20

In addition, you must have five QQ (also called a double Q); that is, you must have competed in at least five different APDT Rally trials where you earned a qualifying score of 190 or above at each level (levels 1 and 2). For instance, when going for your ARCH Championship title, you must enter both levels in each trial and qualify in both levels five times. For example, at the last two trials I entered, Shadow earned a 203 (13 ARCH points) and a 202 (12 ARCH points) in level 1 and a 198 (8 ARCH points) and a 198 (8 ARCH points) in level 2.

The bonus exercises for levels 1 and 2 also go toward your Championship points.

ARCHX Championship Title—To earn the ARCHX title, a team must

➤ Earn the ARCH title.

➤ Earn an additional five QQ's with scores of 195 or above.

There is no restriction on the number of qualifying scores or Rally Championship Title points that may be earned under the same judge in pursuit of ARCH and ARCHX and ARCHEX titles.

ARCHEX Championship Title—To earn the ARCHEX title, a team must

➤ Earn the ARCHX title.

➤ Earn an additional ten QQ's at level 2 and level 3 with scores of 195 or above.

ARCHMX Championship Title — To earn an ARCHMX title, a team must

➤ Earn the ARCHEX title

➤ Earn ten triple Q's in levels 1-2 and level 3 with scores of 195 and above.

Individual level titles go after the dog's name and ARCH, ARCHX, ARCHEX or ARCHMX titles go before the dog's name. For instance, before Shadow got his ARCHEX, the APDT designations for levels 1 and 2 (RL1 and RL2) went after his name. Now that he has finished his ARCHEX, his name looks like this: ARCHEX Ewe Are Beyond a Shadow of a Doubt, CGC, A-CD, NA, NAJ.

AKC TITLE REQUIREMENTS

NOVICE TITLE

➤ Three qualifying scores of 70 or better, earned under two different judges, are required.

➤ The Novice title is designated as RN and appears after the dog's name.

ADVANCED TITLE

➤ Three qualifying scores of 70 or better, earned under two different judges, are required.

➤ The Advanced title is designated as RA and appears after the dog's name.

EXCELLENT TITLE

➤ Three qualifying scores of 70 or better, earned under two different judges, are required.

➤ The Excellent title is designated as RE and appears after the dog's name.

RALLY ADVANCED EXCELLENT TITLE

Upon completion of the Rally Excellent title, qualifying scores may be accumulated from the Rally Advanced B Class and the Rally Excellent B Class to earn the Rally Advanced Excellent (RAE) title.

In order to receive the RAE title, a dog must qualify, at the same trial, in both the Rally Advanced B Class and the Rally Excellent B Class ten times. The RAE title will appear after the dog's name and a numeric designation will indicate the number of times the dog has met RAE requirements, e.g., RAE2, RAE3, etc.

RALLY SIGNS

Please note: At the time of this printing, the information listed here (in terms of exercises in each level and the numbering of each sign) is correct. However, slight changes may occur, so always refer to each venue's website for the most accurate, up-to-date information.

APDT RALLY EXERCISES

LEVEL 1

Level 1 is performed on leash. These are the only signs allowed in level 1. They may also be used in level 2 and 3 courses. A level 1 course consists of 18 to 20 signs, exclusive of the start and finish signs.

Sign	No.	Chapter Discussed
HALT/Sit	#1	4
HALT/Sit/Stand	#2	4
HALT/Sit/Down	#3	4
HALT/Sit/Down/Sit	#4	4
HALT/Sit/Walk Around	#5	4
HALT/Sit/Down/Walk Around	#6	4
Right Turn	#7	3
Left Turn	#8	3
About Turn Right	#9	3
About "U" Turn	#10	3

Sign	No.	Chapter Discussed
270° Right	#11	5
270° Left	#12	5
360° Right	#13	5
360° Left	#14	5
Call Front/Forward Right	#15	4
Call Front/Forward Left	#16	4
Call Front/Finish Right	#17	4
Call Front/Finish Left	#18	4
Slow Pace	#19	4
Fast Pace	#20	4
Normal Pace	#21	4
Moving Side Step Right	#22	5
HALT/90° Pivot Right/HALT	#23	5
HALT/90° Pivot Left/HALT	#24	5
Spiral Right, Dog Outside	#25	5
Spiral Left, Dog Inside	#26	5
HALT/1, 2, 3 Steps Forward	#27	4
HALT/Turn Right/1 Step/HALT	#28	5
Straight Figure 8	#29	5
Serpentine Weave Once	#30	5
Bonus Exercise: Halt/Leave Dog Call to Heel	—	5
Bonus Exercise: Call Front/Sidestep R/L		5
Bonus Exercise: Halt/Leave Dog/Recall Turn and Call/Finish R/L		7

LEVEL 2

Level 2 is performed off leash. The signs listed here may be augmented with signs from level 1 as well. A level 2 course consists of 20 to 22 signs, exclusive of the start and finish signs.

Sign	No.	Chapter Discussed
Off-Set Figure 8	#31	5
Halt Leave Dog	#32	4
Turn/Call to Front (angled) Finish R/L	#33	4

Sign	No.	Chapter Discussed
HALT/Leave Dog/Recall	#34	7
Turn & Call Front	#35	7
Finish Right	#36	7
Finish Left	#37	7
HALT/180° Pivot Right/HALT	#38	5
HALT/180° Pivot Left/HALT	#39	5
HALT/From Sit About Turn Right & Forward	#40	6
HALT/From Sit About "U" Turn & Forward	#41	6
Call Front/1, 2, 3 Steps Backward	#42	4
Send Over Jumps/Handler Runs By	#43	
HALT/Leave/Call Front While Running	#44	6
Moving Down & Forward	#45	4
HALT/Fast Forward From Sit	#46	6
HALT/Side Step Right/HALT	#47	6
Left About Turn	#48	3
Bonus Exercise: Moving Down/Leave Dog (Turn) Call Front/Finish R/L	—	4
Bonus Exercise: Halt Leave Dog/Turn and Down		7
Bonus Exercise: Halt Leave Dog/Turn Call Front (with distractions)		7

LEVEL 3

Level 3 is performed off leash. The signs listed here may be augmented with signs from levels 1 and 2 as well. A Level 3 course consists of 20 to 22 signs, exclusive of the start and finish signs, plus the bonus exercise.

Sign	No.	Chapter Discussed
Moving Stand/Walk Around	#49	7
Moving Stand/Leave Dog	#50	7
Turn and Call to Heel	#51	7
Moving Stand/Leave Dog	#52	7
Turn and Down/Sit/Call/Finish	#53	7
Moving Backup/Heel Back 3 Steps Then Forward	#54	7

Sign	No.	Chapter Discussed
HALT/Leave Dog/Recall Over Jump	#55	7
Turn/Call Over Jump/Finish or Forward	#56	7
HALT/Leave Dog/Send Over Jump	#57	7
Turn and Send Over Jump/Finish or Forward	#58	7
Right Turn/1-2 Steps/Down Dog/Forward	#59	7
Left Turn/1-2 Steps/Down Dog/Forward	#60	7
Halt/Leave Dog/Down on Recall	#61	7
Turn/Recall/Down/Recall/Finish or Forward	#62	7
Call Front/About Turn/Forward	#63	4
Bonus Exercise:		
Turn, HALT, Retrieve, Finish	—	7
Bonus Exercise:		
Call Front/Backup 3 Steps	—	7
Bonus Exercise: Halt/Stand with Distraction		
Return and Forward from Stand	—	6

AKC RALLY EXERCISES

NOVICE

Novice is performed on leash. These are the only signs that may be used in the Novice level. They can also be used in the Advanced and Excellent levels. The average number of exercises used in Novice are 10 to 15.

Sign	No.	Chapter Discussed
Start	#1	—
Finish	#2	—
HALT/Sit	#3	4
HALT/Sit/Down	#4	4
Right Turn	#5	3
Left Turn	#6	3
About Turn Right	#7	3
About "U" Turn	#8	3
270° Right	#9	5
270° Left	#10	5

Sign	No.	Chapter Discussed
360° Right	#11	5
360° Left	#12	5
Call Front/Finish Right/Forward	#13	4
Call Front/Finish Left/Forward	#14	4
Call Front/Finish Right/HALT	#15	4
Call Front/Finish Left/HALT	#16	4
Slow Pace	#17	4
Fast Pace	#18	4
Normal Pace	#19	4
Moving Side Step Right	#20	5
Spiral Right, Dog Outside	#21	5
Spiral Left, Dog Inside	#22	5
Straight Figure 8 Weave Twice	#23	5
Serpentine Weave Once	#24	5
HALT/1, 2, and 3 Steps Forward	#25	4
Call Front/1, 2, and 3 Steps Backward	#26	4
Moving Down/Then Forward	#27	4
HALT/Fast Forward From Sit	#28	6
Left About Turn	#29	3
HALT/Walk Around Dog	#30	4
HALT/Down/Walk Around Dog	#31	4

ADVANCED

Advanced is performed off leash. The signs listed here may be augmented with any number of the signs listed in Novice. Total number of signs that can be used in Advanced are anywhere from 12 to 17.

Sign	No.	Chapter Discussed
HALT/About Turn Right/Forward	#32	6
HALT/About "U" Turn/Forward	#33	6
Send Over Jump/Handler Runs By	#34	6
HALT/Turn Right 1 Step/ Call to Heel/HALT	#35	5
HALT/Stand/Walk Around Dog	#36	4

Sign	No.	Chapter Discussed
HALT/90° Pivot Right/HALT	#37	5
HALT/90° Pivot Left/HALT	#38	5
Off-Set Figure 8	#39	5
HALT/Side Step Right/HALT	#40	6
HALT/Call Dog Front/Finish Right	#41	4
HALT/Call Dog Front/Finish Left	#42	4
HALT/180° Pivot Right/HALT	#43	5
HALT/180° Pivot Left/HALT	#44	5
HALT/Down/Sit	#45	4

EXCELLENT

Excellent is performed off leash. The signs listed here may be augmented with any of the signs listed in the above two levels. There is an average of 15 to 20 exercises in an Excellent course.

Sign	No.	Chapter Discussed
HALT/Stand/Down	#46	4
HALT/Stand/Sit	#47	4
Moving Stand/Walk Around Dog	#48	7
Back Up 3 Steps/Dog Stays in Position	#49	7
Honor Exercise	#50	7

appendix

3

RESOURCES

WEBSITES

American Kennel Club
www.akc.org

This website lists the AKC rules and regulations for Rally trials, and has information on seminars throughout the country. Many of the forms you need are here as well as Rally signs you can print out.

Association of Pet Dog Trainers
www.apdt.com

This website lists when and where Rally trials, matches, classes and seminars are being held throughout the country. You can also find Rally rules and regulations here and the national ranking for APDT Rally. Many of the forms you need also are here, as well as signs you can print out.

J & J Dog Supplies
www.jjdog.com

If you don't want to print out your own signs, J & J is the only place (at the time of this printing) that sells the equipment you will need (laminated signs, metal holders, stakes, as well as cones, bowls with screens, etc.).

Sit Stay Go Out
www.sitstaygoout.com

This is a good source of training equipment, books, videos and treats.

Black Ice Dog Sledding

www.blackicedogsledding.com

Here is another harness source—very helpful people, a great and comfortable harness. This harness is for dogs of any size, although I like it better on smaller dogs (50 pounds and under). Measure twice, order once. The harness is not adjustable.

Match Show Bulletin

www.matchshowbulletin.com

This newsletter lists many of the matches, seminars, trials and classes on the East Coast for many dog sports.

Front and Finish Magazine

www.frontandfinish.com

This magazine is considered the news for dog trainers. *Front & Finish* has been the foundation of information in dog obedience and other canine performance events for over thirty years!

Clean Run Productions

www.cleanrun.com

Besides selling *Clean Run* magazine and their own dog agility training books and videos, they offer a broad spectrum of dog toys, dog treats, dog training equipment, and all sorts of products for dog agility training and trialing, dog obedience training, flyball training, clicker training, and just having fun with your dog.

Dogwise

www.dogwise.com

An excellent website for the titles listed below.

BOOKS

Bones Would Rain From the Sky, by Suzanne Clothier (Warner Books, 2005).

Explore the dog-human relationship with this book.

Bringing Light to Shadow: A Dog Trainer's Diary, by Pamela Dennison (Dogwise Publishing, 2005).

Pam's mistakes and successes come to life in a diary that tells of a successful achievement with her aggressive dog, bringing hope to owners of similar types of dogs.

On Talking Terms with Dogs: Calming Signals (video and book), by Turid Rugaas (Dogwise Publishing, 2005).

Dogs do have a language and it isn't English! Watch this four times a week for at least a month.

Civilizing the City Dog by Pamela Dennison with Jolanta Benal (Alpine Publications, 2007)

For those of you that live in a more urban environment, this is the continuation to *How to Right a Dog Gone Wrong*.

Clicker Training for Obedience (competition), by Morgan Spector (Sunshine Books, 1998).

If you're interested in training competition obedience, here is a good resource using positive training methods.

The Complete Idiot's Guide to Positive Dog Training, by Pamela Dennison (2nd ed., Alpha Books, 2006).

Here is your basic positive training manual, containing positive training methods as well as background information on the hows and whys of positive training. Tons of step-by-step instructions are included for teaching behaviors and getting rid of unwanted behaviors.

Conquering Ring Nerves, by Diane Peters Mayer (Howell Book House, 2004).

This is a "must have" book if you are planning on competing.

Culture Clash, by Jean Donaldson (James & Kenneth, 1996).

This is one of the best books on the market—I only wish I had written it! This book has shaped modern thinking about canine behavior and the relationship between dogs and humans.

Dominance: Fact or Fiction? by Barry Eaton (self-published, 2005).

This neat little booklet dispels the myths about dominance theory.

Excel-erated Learning, by Pamela Reid (James & Kenneth, 1996).

Here's more information for you on how to teach and how dogs learn.

How to Right a Dog Gone Wrong: A Roadmap for Rehabilitating Aggressive Dogs, by Pamela Dennison (Alpine Publications, 2005).

Re-train your wayward pooch with the positive methods outlined in this book.

How to Speak Dog, by Stanley Coren (Fireside Books, 2000).

This super book explains the whys and wherefores of the body postures dogs display for increased understanding of your canine companion.

The Other End of the Leash, by Patricia McConnell (Ballantine Books, 2002).

This excellent canine behavioral study is written by a top animal behaviorist.

ABOUT THE AUTHOR

When Pam Dennison watched the demo dogs in her first training class, she knew within minutes that competition obedience was going to be in her future. The beauty and rhythm as the dog mirrored his owner's every move took her breath away.

Pam started competing in 1996 and qualified and competed in the Eastern United States Dog Obedience Championships in 1997. After switching from traditional punishment-based training methods to positive ones, she started her own obedience school, Positive Motivation Dog Training, in 1997. At present she lives with two rescued dogs (Border Collies). She began competing in APDT Rally in 2003 and is completely hooked on the sport. Her dogs have earned many titles to date, spanning Competition obedience, Rally obedience, and Agility. Pam is continuing to compete for more titles in these sports, as well as train for sheepherding, tracking, and carting. To date, her students have earned a multitude of titles and certificates in obedience,

Pam with Beau, ARCHEX Surely Ewe Beau Jest, CGC, TDI, CD, A-UD, NAJP, NAP, TSW. Photo: Paul Zurka.

Rally, tracking, and sheep herding, plus many qualifications for Canine Good Citizen and Therapy Dog certification.

Pam teaches puppy kindergarten, beginners, Canine Good Citizen, Musical Freestyle, Rally and Competition classes at her facility in Belvidere, New Jersey. She works with all breeds, from Dachshunds to Great Danes and every size in between. Pam holds behavior modification classes for aggressive and reactive dogs, as well as seminars and camps based on her work with Shadow, called Camp R.E.W.A.R.D.

She is the author of *The Complete Idiot's Guide to Positive Dog Training*, Alpha Books, *Bringing Light to Shadow; A Dog Trainer's Diary*, Dogwise Publishing, *How to Right a Dog Gone Wrong; A Roadmap for Rehabilitating Aggressive Dogs*, Alpine Publications, and *Civilizing the City Dog*, Alpine Publications. Pam also has four videos available: *Camp R.E.WA.R.D. for Aggressive Dogs* and *Positive Solutions for Standard Behavioral Problems*, both from Barkleigh Productions, *The Magic of Shaping; Explore the Possibilities*, Tawzer Dog Videos, and *Training the Whistle Recall*, (Winner of the 2009 Maxwell Award for Best Training Video) available from the author. Pam is a member of the APDT (Association of Pet Dog Trainers) and the DWAA (Dog Writers Association of America), and is a Certified Dog Behavior Consultant with the IAABC (International Association of Animal Behavior Consultants).

Pam has published many articles in national and international magazines and speaks on a myriad of topics relating to positive training, Rally, competition obedience, shaping and aggression. She can be reached through her website: www.positivedogs.com.

Pam with Shadow, ARCHEX Ewe
Are Beyond a Shadow of a
Doubt, CGC, A-CD, NAJ, NA, TSW.

Photo: Paul Zurka

If you liked

Click Your Way to Rally

you might also be interested in. . .

THE RALLY COURSE BOOK

Janice Dearth

Created to help exhibitors, instructors and judges design, set up, and judge AKC Rally, this book includes useable course designs with exhibitor sheets. Spiral bound to lay flat for reference. Updated through July 2010. Paperback, 96 pages with diagrams. List price $24.95

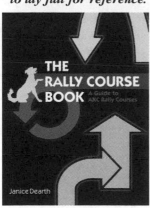

BUILDING BLOCKS FOR PERFORMANCE

Bobbie Anderson and Tracy Libby

Start your puppy on the path to the winners circle with positive training exercises, play training, motivation and more. Develop that winning attitude and competitive spirit needed for any performance event. Softcover, 144 pages, illustrated. List price $29.95

Helping you succeed with horses and dogs!
For a current listing of book titles, visit us at:
www.alpinepub.com